Integrity at Stake

SAFEGUARDING YOUR CHURCH'S HONOR

Rollie Dimos

Rollie Dimos
1830 N. 23rd St.
Ozark, MO 65721
web address: www.RollieDimos.com

Ordering Information:
Special discounts are available on quantity purchases. For ordering details, contact the
publisher at the address above.

ISBN: 978-0-9961076-0-0

Printed in United States of America.

For my wife and best friend, Tammy.
*Thank you for being my biggest fan
and cheerleader.*
*I couldn't have accomplished this book
without your constant support and encouragement.*

For my parents.
*As leaders in the church,
you consistently modeled accountability,
transparency and integrity.*

CONTENTS

foreword

The church, parachurch and non-profit organizations are designed to be conduits of hope and rays of light that result in the transformation of people's lives.

However, when an organization neglects good stewardship practices, it can lead to fraud and financial abuse. When this occurs, it diminishes that ministry's Kingdom influence.

There have been some improprieties that are so acute, that the government is actually wondering if churches and nonprofits are complying with the law. All of this causes the church and the ministry to lose credibility and ultimately its ministry effectiveness.

If there is one thing better than a minister of a church or a CEO of a nonprofit organization publicly admitting mistakes and asking for forgiveness, it's NOT having to have a public reading of any transgressions!

My friend and colleague, Rollie Dimos, has devoted his life to helping Christ-centered organizations earn and maintain high levels of trust, through developing high standards of accountability and practice. He gets it...both the ministry and management!

Integrity at Stake is not a fictional book. These are actual situations that caused financial setback and were embarrassing to the ministry. Interestingly, each of these could have been avoided if greater accountability and transparency were embedded in the ministry's policy and practice.

Caution: the subject material in this book may prevent you from experiencing any fraudulent schemes in the ministry you lead!

Doug Clay | *General Treasurer*
The Assemblies of God National Leadership and Resource Center

introduction

The biblical patriarch Job understood adversity. He knew despair. He had experienced loss of health, loss of family and loss of fortune. In the midst of unfathomable grief and loss, his wife and friends were encouraging him to turn his back on God. However, Job didn't waver in his convictions. He understood his character was on the line.

His integrity was at stake.

Job was pressured to compromise, but he stood firm in his convictions and didn't sin against God. He maintained his integrity, and he maintained his honor.

I've been involved in the financial operations of various churches and nonprofits for almost twenty-five years. From performing the bookkeeping, to being elected treasurer, and providing consulting services to pastors and boards as an internal auditor, I've been involved in all aspects of a ministry's financial operations. I've served alongside ministries with good financial practices, and I've been able to help other ministries improve poor practices.

But over the years, I've seen people who, unlike Job, compromised their integrity and committed financial abuses. Abuses that included:

- Pastors and bookkeepers writing church checks to pay for personal expenses for their family and friends.
- Church staff using the church credit card for personal charges.
- Pastors hiding unauthorized transactions from the board.

- Ministry leaders transferring funds to secret bank accounts.
- Churches that had to close their doors because they failed to send their payroll taxes to the IRS.

The world is suffering an economic crisis—and our churches are not immune to this crisis either. We often think that fraud only happens on Wall Street, but, sadly, it also happens on Main Street—in the midst of our churches.

We may think that organizational fraud is a victimless crime—since the organization isn't a real person, and companies should have sufficient funds to recover the loss. However, when fraud occurs in the church, significant spiritual ramifications linger long after the financial. The church will have probably lost some funds, but a financial abuse performed by a spiritual leader can ruin the leader's ministry and possibly destroy a church, leaving a building full of people whose faith has been shattered in its wake.

Misuse and abuse of ministry funds occur due to the lack of accountability—in some of the cases mentioned earlier, accountability was virtually nonexistent.

I encourage churches to embrace accountability and transparency, two essential keys that will minimize risk and help your church fulfill its mission. And by adding a few simple internal controls, you will increase the accountability and transparency of your nonprofit organization, bring integrity to your financial operations, and in my opinion, characterize biblical stewardship!

But everyone in the church must embrace accountability and transparency. These two keys must be part of your church culture and DNA. Most importantly, they must be modeled by your leadership. And, pastors, as you model accountability and transparency in your churches, your staff, church board, and congregation will follow!

Over the next few chapters, I'll discuss the importance of accountability in your ministry's financial operations, and reveal the impact that poor controls have had on various churches and nonprofits.

I pray that as you read though this book, you'll understand how embracing accountability and transparency will help the success of your ministry and protect your church's honor.

who should read this book

Within every organization, someone has the primary task of managing the organization's finances. No matter the title—bookkeeper, accountant, treasurer, or chief financial officer—these people have the day-to-day responsibility of receiving income, paying bills, recording transactions, and preparing financial reports. Certainly, they also have a responsibility to make sure assets are safeguarded and proper controls are in place to minimize the risk of fraud.

However, this book is also written for many others within the organization who are charged with the responsibility to steward non-profit resources and prevent the misuse and abuse of donor funds, including:

- Pastor/president. As pastor, you may also fulfill the role of president, chairman of the board, or chief executive officer. You probably don't count the offering, make deposits, or post transactions into the financial records, but you decide when and where funds are spent. You also have the authority to bypass established policies, which sometimes circumvents controls. This book is for you to help you realize the importance of implementing and enforcing a system of internal control.
- Treasurer/chief financial officer. Your role includes managing the financial operations and providing reports on the current status of finances. It is important for you

to know financial controls are in place and operating effectively.

- Accounting staff. Whether your title is accountant, bookkeeper, finance specialist, or accounting clerk, you handle the day-to-day financial transactions for the organization. The accuracy and integrity of the organization's finances rests with the accounting team.
- Deacon/board of directors. Your role, as the governing board, includes making sure finances are managed effectively while propelling the organization forward in fulfilling its mission. You'll want to make sure segregation of duties and other financial controls are in place to safeguard the organization's assets while protecting the integrity of the organization and its staff.

Essentially, every employee in the church or non-profit ministry plays a part in preventing fraud. No matter your title or role, this book will reveal how fraud can occur in churches and other nonprofit organizations, and how you can prevent it.

everyone in the church

must embrace

accountability

and transparency

SECTION ONE

Fraud

A FRANK DISCUSSION

ON THE POTENTIAL

RISKS TO YOUR

ORGANIZATION

CHAPTER ONE

FRAUD RISK: WHAT EVERY LEADER NEEDS TO KNOW

facing the facts

Y ou might have read this headline in 2009: "Father and son pastors plead guilty to stealing $3.1 million from church."[1] Or maybe you read about the pastor who embezzled $700,000 from his congregation[2], or that $1.3 million designated for church planting was misused by pastors.[3]

Many times, we think that fraud only happens in large corporations like Enron or WorldCom, but it can happen to small nonprofit organizations, too. Unfortunately, many religious and charitable organizations may think their organizations aren't at risk because they employ people who, they feel, possess strong moral and ethical convictions. Others may erroneously believe that strong controls require additional staff and great expense. As a result, leaders let their guard down and fail to implement processes with strong controls.

One of the most frequent abuses in church finances is using nonprofit funds for personal use by stealing cash from the offering plate, writing unauthorized checks, or using the church credit card for personal expenses. External pressures such as personal debt, medical crisis, or an unexpected job loss can cause even the most loyal employee to make a rash and unfortunate decision. These perpetrators may rationalize their actions by thinking of it as just a temporary loan, fully intending to pay it back. Others justify their actions because they feel underpaid or undervalued and believe they are owed the extra pay.

In 2012, the Association of Certified Fraud Examiners examined 1,388 fraud cases, of which 10.4 percent occurred at nonprofit organizations.[4] First-time offenders, with no prior criminal records, perpetrated the fraud in 87 percent of all cases.[5] For those non-profit organizations that experienced fraud, the median loss was $100,000.[6]

If a fraud occurs, the church will lose more than just money. Donor confidence will rightly be weakened, and they may decide to reallocate their contributions to other organizations. Further, the reputation of the church and its pastor in the local community could be permanently damaged.

Can your church afford a loss of this magnitude? More importantly, do you know how to protect your organization from fraud?

interest from all sides

Accountability and transparency shouldn't be exercised just for the donors in the pews, but are also important to the many other organizations watching you.

Certainly donors want to make sure their contributions to a particular ministry are used responsibly and further the ministry's stated goals. But external interests also monitor the accountability and good governance of nonprofits.

Media and watchdog groups keep a watchful eye on nonprofit activity to ensure it is transparent and responsible. State attorneys general are interested in protecting the funds donated by their constituents, and the IRS requires that nonprofits comply with appropriate rules and regulations for tax-exempt groups. In fact, from 2002 to 2012, the percentage of tax-exempt returns examined by the IRS has doubled.[7]

Congress also watches to make sure religious organizations are accountable and compliant to maintain public confidence in the nonprofit sector. In January 2011, Senator Chuck Grassley, ranking member of the Committee on Finance, released a report on the review of activities and practices of media-based ministries, churches, and other religious organizations. Characterized as an ongoing effort to strengthen the tax-exempt sector, Grassley said his goal was to improve accountability and governance of tax-exempt organizations in order to maintain public confidence.[8]

why accountability matters

Often times, I meet church leaders who are fearful of making their financial activity accountable and transparent, and many times, control of the church's finances is limited to one or two individuals. In a best-case scenario, this is simply an honest, but naive mind-set believing that finances are better controlled when fewer people are involved. In a worst-case scenario, this is a deliberate attempt to conceal poor stewardship or abuse. It's the worst-case scenario that will ruin a leader's ministry, destroy a church, and shatter people's faith.

A prominent preacher once lamented publicly that accountability is just a code name for red tape. He stated that it was simply a tool for accountants and bureaucrats to question a leader's decisions and a back-door approach for stopping progress. It was apparent this leader wasn't a fan of accountability and transparency. Unfortunately, a few years later, this leader learned that his associate pastor had embezzled $700,000 from the church. The associate pastor's decision to steal from the church was his own choosing; however, the lack of accountability in the organization was certainly a contributing factor.

This type of situation can be avoided by embracing accountability—and by realizing that accountability is a scriptural principle!

The principle of accountability runs throughout the Bible. In scriptural terms, accountability means giving an account of how well we steward the gifts and resources that God gives us. The Parable of the Talents is an example of how God holds us accountable for our stewardship (Matthew 25:14–30). And as described in the Book of Revelation, each person will stand before God and give an individual accounting of their lives on the Day of Judgment (Revelation 20:11–15; see also Romans 14:12).

Paul even addresses the accountability of his work in his letter to the Corinthian church. He wrote: "We want to avoid any criticism of the way we administer this liberal gift. For we are taking pains to do what is right, not only in the eyes of the Lord but also in the eyes of men" (2 Corinthians 8:20–21).

In business terms, church leaders are the stewards of an organization's resources, including all funds received from donors. Pastors and board members are accountable to one another for the business decisions they make. And they are all accountable to their donors for how well they steward contributions.

In practical terms, without accountability, human nature tends to drive us to the dividing line between right and wrong, where we encounter the gray areas of life. Certainly, making right choices involves listening to the leading of the Holy Spirit; but it also involves submitting ourselves to others and seeking wise counsel. The Book of Proverbs reminds us that "in the multitude of counsellors there is safety" (Proverbs 11:14, KJV).

In today's world, leaders feel pressured to follow the latest trends and buzz words. They are strongly encouraged to try new things, push the envelope, think outside the box, and engage the current culture and ideas. Ideas are not intrinsically evil; and in many cases, they may be necessary to foster a growing and thriving congregation. But without submitting ourselves to another's accountability, anyone could more easily cross the line into misuse and abuse.

Accountability and transparency of financial operations aren't meant to constrain leaders, but they are, instead, meant to protect leaders and the reputations of their organizations. If I could paraphrase that verse from Proverbs: Where there is a multitude of counselors *who discuss, review, and approve the financial operations of the church*, there truly is safety.

We are taking pains to do what is right,

not only in the eyes of the Lord

but also in the eyes of men.

CHAPTER TWO

INTERNAL CONTROL
&
RISK MANAGEMENT

forging a strong defense

The economic downturn in recent years has affected many organizations' ability to meet their business goals. Maybe you were an employee of a manufacturing company who experienced production cutbacks, reduced hours, layoffs, or even termination. Maybe you have family members or close friends who have experienced a recent job loss. Undoubtedly, the economic condition has affected many of us.

But what about churches and other nonprofit organizations? How has the economic crisis affected them? More importantly, has the country's economic downturn impacted the risk of fraud in our churches?

Consider these statistics:

- A survey published in 2013 by the Leadership Network found 50 percent of churches were negatively impacted by the economy in recent years. Not surprising, they discovered church size was directly proportional to the amount of negative impact experienced. For example, 67 percent of churches with less than 1,000 in attendance were negatively impacted by the economy.[9]
- A recent study of fraud events identified in 2012 found that 65 percent of fraudsters were motivated by a desire to increase or maintain their standard of living.[10]
- Another study of fraud investigated between 2008 and 2011 determined that the perpetrator experienced financial difficulties in 31.5 percent of the cases between

2008 and 2009, and 27 percent of the cases between 2010 and 2011.[11]

These statistics reveal the real risk that our churches face. Financial pressures on our church members mean increased pressure in our churches. Strong internal controls are an effective defense to the increased risk of fraud in our churches, and they are a key component of risk management.

Simply put, risk management is the process of identifying, evaluating, and responding to uncertainties (i.e., corporate risk) that could jeopardize an organization's ability to achieve their business objectives.

To understand why risk management is important to your organization, consider two key terms in that definition: corporate risk and business objectives.

Corporate risk, or business risk, refers to potential sources of trouble that businesses face. These are the types of risks that, if they occurred, would impact the success of your organization. Unfortunately, churches are not immune to corporate risk, which could include:

- Not meeting ministry goals
- Misusing designated funds
- Using nonprofit funds contrary to IRS regulations
- Financial misconduct by staff
- Reduced contributions (through increased economic pressure on donors or by losing donor confidence and trust)

Business objectives are those short-term and long-term goals that define how your organization will achieve its mission. Together, these objectives help create a roadmap for the future. Here are some examples of a church's business objectives:

- Accountable and transparent operations
- Biblical stewardship of donor resources
- Strong donor confidence
- Safeguarded assets

Business objectives may be perpetual (never-ending), as in the examples used above, or they may be short-lived; for example, "increase capital funds by ten percent in twelve months."

You may find the business objectives of a local church in its mission statement, or they may be found in a list of the church's core values. For example, the mission statement of the Assemblies of God Fellowship is to fulfill the four-fold mission of the church: evangelism, worship, discipleship, and compassion. Further, the fellowship will fulfill this mission by committing to the following five core values:

- Passionately proclaim Jesus as Savior
- Strategically invest in the next generation
- Vigorously plant new churches
- Skillfully resource the church
- Fervently pray for God's favor[12]

While the fellowship implements these five core values, they will need to effectively identify, evaluate, and respond to various uncertainties and risk factors that could hinder their ability to achieve their four-fold mission.

The success of the business objectives and core values of your organization will also be directly affected by your organization's response to risk. Our challenge as leaders is to first identify the risks, and then decide on a plan of action to manage the controllable risks and minimize the uncontrollable risks.

This is the relationship between risk management and internal controls. Your organization's system of internal control is your first line of defense to combat the risks that could hinder the success of your mission.

finding holes in the defense

A survey completed by KPMG International in 2011 found that 74 percent of the fraud cases that they reviewed occurred by exploiting weak internal controls.[13] KPMG theorized that due to a downturn in the economy, many organizations had to cut costs to balance their finances. These cost-cutting measures resulted in less robust controls and few resources to monitor those controls. This allowed fraudsters to exploit the weaknesses.

Unfortunately, the average fraud in North American companies occurred repeatedly for over four years before being detected, and the average loss exceeded $1.2 million.[14] In 96 percent of these cases, the perpetrator conducted repeated fraudulent activity, which raises the question of whether the controls for detecting and preventing fraud were effective, and whether management was performing adequate oversight.[15]

For nonprofits, the statistics are just as alarming.

The Association of Certified Fraud Examiner's 2012 *Report to the Nations* is a must-read for church leaders who are interested in minimizing the risk of fraud and embezzlement in their organization. From January 2010 to December 2011, the ACFE reviewed 1,388 cases of worldwide occupational fraud. Here are some interesting findings from the report:

- The typical organization loses 5 percent of its revenue to fraud each year.
- The median loss for fraud cases reviewed was $140,000, but more than 20 percent had actual losses greater than $1 million.
- The smallest organizations in the study suffered the largest median losses; they had the least amount of anti-fraud controls making them more vulnerable to fraud.
- Frauds committed by owners and executives was significantly larger than frauds committed by managers and employees.
- Over 80 percent of the fraudsters exhibited behavioral red flags, such as living beyond their means, experiencing financial difficulties, or had unusually close relationships with customers or vendors.[16]

Unfortunately, churches and ministry organizations are not immune to fraudulent activity. Of the 1,388 fraud cases reviewed, 10.4 percent occurred within non-profit organizations.[17] The median loss for non-profit organizations was $100,000 while strictly religious and charitable organizations experienced a median loss of $85,000.[18]

Often times, fraud schemes are difficult to detect and usually involve people who you'd least suspect. According to the ACFE, fraud schemes lasted a median of eighteen months before being detected.[19] And in 87 percent of all cases reviewed, the perpetrator was a first-time offender with no prior criminal record and 84 percent had a clean employment history.[20]

However, strong internal controls and other accountability measures can help detect fraud sooner. For those organizations that had implemented various internal controls, the frauds were detected sooner and resulted in less monetary losses. The ACFE found:

- 43 percent of frauds were uncovered through tips.
- 29 percent of frauds were uncovered by internal reviews (management reviews and internal audits).
- 9 percent of frauds were uncovered by reconciling accounts and examining support documents.[21]

Somewhat surprising, the ACFE determined only 3 percent of frauds were uncovered by external audits.[22] Unfortunately, I find many churches rely on a financial statement audit as their only fraud detection tool.

Some of the characteristics discussed above are the very reasons that our churches are at risk for fraud. Churches often have only one or two people involved in the accounting and bookkeeping functions. Financial controls are usually vested in just one or two people. Budgets are tight, so fewer resources are invested in strengthening financial controls. Often, the pastor has significant authority and influence over financial activity.

The ACFE study revealed that small businesses, like churches, are particularly vulnerable to fraud. The ACFE concluded:

> These organizations typically have fewer resources than their larger counterparts, which often translates to fewer and less-effective anti-fraud controls. In addition, because they have fewer resources, the losses experienced by small businesses tend to have a greater impact than they would in larger organizations.[23]

The ACFE estimates that 5 percent of an organization's revenues are lost to fraud. But the cost of fraud is particularly harmful to small organizations like churches—where the actual impact will not only include finances, but a damaged reputation and a loss of donor confidence.

In 2011, public charities reported over 1.5 trillion dollars in total revenues.[24] If five percent is lost to fraud each year, this equates to over 75 billion dollars lost to fraud in 2011. Think about the magnitude of that statistic: Public charities lost access to over 75 billion dollars that couldn't be used to further their charitable causes around the world.

The good news is that the organizations that implemented any number of common anti-fraud controls experienced lower losses than organizations that didn't implement these controls. The duration of the fraud was considerably less as well. The implication for churches is clear: Even though they may have fewer resources at their disposal, churches and other non-profits must implement measures to reduce the risk of fraud in their organizations. Strong controls like segregation of duties, robust reviews and approvals, and transparency are a must.

defining internal control

Have you heard the phrase: "Inspect what you expect"? When discussing U.S. relations with the Soviet Union, President Ronald Reagan often quoted a similar Russian proverb, "doveryai no proveryai," or "trust, but verify."[25]

These phrases succinctly convey the role internal control plays in minimizing risk within nonprofit organizations.

According to COSO[26], internal control is a process to provide reasonable assurance that an organization will have:

- Effective and efficient operations
- Reliable financial reports
- Compliance with applicable laws and regulations[27]

Everyone would probably agree that these are three great business objectives for the local church. But they are not confined to the finance and accounting function; they encompass the broader business goals of the organization.

One of the most important financial controls within an organization is the segregation of duties. This is a key component of internal control that involves multiple people. This is especially important when handling cash. I like to summarize this control as requiring two sets of eyes on every transaction—from collecting and counting the offering, to recording the deposits, to paying the bills. A system of internal control also includes establishing goals and objectives, creating operating policies and procedures, organizing and training staff, etc.

Internal control helps ensure that the "business of ministry" is successful. In other words, internal control is a process for managing risk!

taking ownership

In the nonprofit world, the purpose of internal control is to increase the accountability, transparency, and integrity of financial operations. This goes hand in hand with the biblical theme of stewardship.

Unfortunately, sometimes leaders view internal control as roadblocks or obstacles. Remember, many nonprofits are vulnerable to fraud or abuse because they have a weak system of controls, but let me challenge your thinking and submit to you that a system of internal control actually helps promote biblical stewardship of God's resources! Internal control will reduce the risks of financial loss, the risks of not meeting business goals, and the risks of losing donor confidence.

In my experience, two key causes of weak controls are prevalent in our churches today: poor segregation of duties and frequent override of established policies and procedures. These can be easily overcome—and without significant cost, additional staff, or time. But it requires the leadership to recognize the importance of, and commit to, strong controls.

Think about your church or ministry organization and answer these questions:

- What is the ethical climate of your organization (i.e. "tone at the top")?
- Are your leaders characterized as those who make exceptions to policy or follow policy?
- Are accountability and transparency practiced at all levels of your organization?

Internal control is only effective as a risk management tool if everyone is supporting it, including the president and board members, full-time staff, and part-time staff. From the boardroom to the mailroom, everyone is responsible for internal control.

Let me encourage you to practice accountability through the implementation of strong internal control processes. This will include publicly embracing accountability, documenting specific internal controls in your policies and procedures manuals, and embedding this theme throughout your organization's DNA. I said this earlier, but it is worth repeating again: Pastors, as you model accountability in your churches, your staff and congregation will follow!

Later in this book, I'll discuss several real-life examples of how weak systems of internal control contributed to fraud and abuse in different ministry organizations. (While all of these stories are true, the names of the individuals and organizations involved have been changed to protect their identities.)

If you find your organization is similar to one or more of these case studies, having similar processes and practicing weak controls,

I'll provide several ways to implement additional measures that will improve controls and reduce the risk of fraud within your organization.

From the boardroom

to the mailroom,

everyone is responsible

for internal control.

CHAPTER THREE

MOVING FORWARD AFTER FRAUD

the consequences of fraud

Fraud is not a victimless crime; all of the frauds discussed in this book were not harmless acts, but had dire consequences for the defrauded organizations. If your church has been a victim of a fraud, you are well aware of these consequences.

As previously stated, when fraud occurs in the church, there are spiritual consequences as well as financial. The church can lose more than just money. It can end up ruining a leader's ministry, destroying a church, and shattering people's faith. It also impacts the organization's ability to perform ministry and meet the needs of others.

Consider the consequences that the following organizations faced:

- One church that was the victim of a $712,000 embezzlement scheme by their office manager had to cut employee's pay by 10 percent and cancel a benevolence assistance program for their members.[28]
- A Catholic archdiocese that was defrauded of one million dollars by their accounts payable clerk had to close churches and schools because funds designated for Catholic education were stolen.[29]
- An employee of the American Diabetes Association embezzled nearly $570,000 from the Association. Instead of helping the twenty-five million Americans who have this disease, the stolen funds were spent at casinos, restaurants, and clothing stores.[30]

- A church treasurer who defrauded a Las Vegas church out of 1.75 million dollars caused the church to lose their property to foreclosure.[31]

There are several ways to reduce the risk of fraud in your organization. Taking action before fraud occurs is certainly the wisest choice and would include proactive measures such as training or awareness campaigns and implementing internal control to increase accountability and transparency.

However, if you experience fraud at your organization, the actions you take will directly impact the risk of future frauds occurring. These reactive measures would include fixing the process or control weakness that allowed the fraud to occur, taking disciplinary action on the person who committed the abuse, and making other employees aware that abuse of ministry funds will not be tolerated.

taking disciplinary action

While disciplinary action is reactive—meaning it is taken after a fraud occurs—it can also be a proactive measure. Taking disciplinary action will let others know that fraudulent behavior will not be tolerated and can discourage others from participating in abuse in the future.

While a major tenant of the Church involves forgiveness, it is important to remember that fraud is a serious crime; the perpetrator has broken the law and breached a sacred trust. Richard Hammar, a legal expert in church and clergy issues, offers the following advice to church leaders when they find someone has committed a fraud:

- Find out how much money was actually taken (hire a local certified public accountant or certified fraud examiner, if necessary).
- Require full restitution of the funds within a specified period of time.
- Have the embezzler sign a promissory note, detailing the amount to pay and the specified period of time.
- Permanently remove the embezzler from any position within the church that involves handling money.[32]

The question on whether to turn the case over to the police or local prosecutor is a question that each organization will have to answer for itself based on the circumstances of the case. This may also be necessary if the suspected embezzler doesn't confess or it isn't clear who is guilty.[33]

The answer may also involve the severity of the fraud and the ability and willingness of the perpetrator to make restitution. As Hammar points out, since the embezzler probably didn't report the stolen funds as income, "in some cases it is more likely that the IRS will prosecute the embezzler for tax evasion than the local prosecutor will prosecute for the crime of embezzlement."[34]

Let me illustrate this by elaborating on two of the stories that will be discussed later in this book.

- A trusted volunteer was buying personal items at a local supermarket and charging those purchases to the church. After the volunteer was caught at the supermarket trying to make another fraudulent purchase, she was taken to the police station. The church decided not to prosecute if the volunteer made restitution. However, the volunteer was removed from her position and not allowed to volunteer for a period of time. She was repentant, and she made restitution over the next eighteen months. Although she was not allowed to hold any position in the church that involved handling money, she was restored to fellowship within the congregation. The woman and her husband remained active in the church for several years. (pages 80–83)

- The office manager of a nonprofit organization was caught using blank checks to make personal purchases for herself and her family. The organization initiated an internal investigation to determine the scope of her theft, but didn't prosecute. In fact, they allowed the office manager to resign, instead of being fired, and didn't require restitution. She moved out of town and found another job as a bookkeeper at a church. While the church was checking her references, they called the previous employer for a recommendation and were only told that she resigned. Unfortunately for that church, the bookkeeper continued her fraudulent ways and was caught misusing funds again. (pages 70–73)

These two stories highlight the different paths that organizations can take when they catch a trusted employee or volunteer stealing funds. In one case, the perpetrator was required to make restitution and went through a successful period of rehabilitation. In the other case, the perpetrator was allowed to resign and move on without any consequences. Unfortunately, this didn't stop the perpetrator's fraudulent ways.

The dichotomy of these two outcomes would suggest that taking some sort of disciplinary action is more effective in stopping a person from continuing their abuse at another organization.

However, not all organizations take significant disciplinary action.

According to the ACFE, 87 percent of occupational fraudsters have never been charged or convicted of fraud and 84 percent have never been fired for fraud-related conduct.[35] While this indicates that many fraudsters are first-time offenders, I believe it also indicates that employers do not always press charges against employees who steal. As a result, they are able to commit abuses at their next employer.

But statistics are somewhat encouraging for those organizations that do take action. The ACFE study found that when an organization experienced fraud, 65 percent referred the case for criminal prosecution, while 24 percent filed a civil lawsuit instead of criminal action.[36]

When cases were referred to law enforcement for criminal prosecution, 72 percent of the perpetrators plead guilty or were convicted.[37]

When a civil lawsuit was pursued, 80 percent received a judgment in favor of the organization or reached a settlement.[38]

Unfortunately, while a majority received a favorable judgment, their research also indicates that 40 to 50 percent of organizations do not recover any of their losses.[39]

It's understandable that churches and nonprofits have a difficult time with a decision to prosecute or not. When organizations didn't refer a fraud case to law enforcement, the most often cited reason was the fear of bad publicity.[40]

Airing dirty laundry isn't a pleasant thought. It reveals your current processes were weak and allowed the abuse to occur. It may reveal that leaders weren't performing adequate oversight. It will also let donors know that their contributions didn't further the ministry of the organization, but were used to line the pockets of someone they trusted.

Fear of bad publicity is a valid concern. Details of the scandal may be publicized on the front page of the local newspaper and may be the lead story on the evening news. Members may lose confidence in the ministry's ability to effectively perform their stated goals and donors may move their funds elsewhere.

However, let me caution you that a decision to not take action may be just as harmful in the long run. In today's world of social media, instant communication and constant connections, it is inevitable that news of the scandal will become known. While fear of bad publicity is normal, trying to hide bad news or "sweeping it under the rug" may be just as damaging.

the power of the audit

One way to ensure your processes, procedures, and controls are robust enough to prevent fraud from happening in your organization is to put them through the scrutiny of an audit. There are a few different types of audits that can be performed, from assessing the strength of your controls, to opining on the reasonableness of your financial statements. These audits can also be performed by knowledgeable businessmen and -women in your congregation or by an independent public accounting firm.

Before you decide on what type of audit you need or who will perform it, you should decide what your needs are. For example, do you need accurate financial statements to present to your board, congregation, or banking institution? Do you need to review your internal processes to assess compliance with your policies and procedures? Do you need to evaluate the effectiveness of a specific function in the church like payroll or accounts payable?

Additionally, you need to consider what funding and resources are available. Do you have qualified businessmen or -women within your congregation who are willing and available to perform a review? Do you have a trusted relationship with a local public accounting firm? Do you have available funding to pay for an in-depth audit?

Finally, you should review your constitution and bylaws. This document may have specific language regarding the type of audit required and how often it should be completed. Your bylaws may require audited financial statements annually, which would indicate an audit by a public accounting firm. However, if your bylaws only require a review of your finances on a regular basis, this could indicate a review by qualified businessmen and -women in the organization would suffice.

Your specific needs will dictate the type of audit that should be performed.

A financial statement audit is performed by an independent

public accounting firm (called an external audit). The public accounting firm will ensure your organization's financial statements comply with generally accepted accounting principles (GAAP), and a certified public accountant (CPA) will express an opinion on whether those financial statements are relevant, complete, and fairly presented.

The focus of the public accounting firm is very specific. The accounting firm will focus on the presentation of the financial statements and compliance with GAAP. They will perform specific tests of internal controls and gather sufficient evidence to base their opinion. They will focus on material errors—those errors that will result in a misstatement of the financial statements and affect the decisions of informed readers of those financial statements.

By choosing a financial statement audit, your church is choosing to compare your financial management reporting and processes to generally accepted accounting principles. This means that many of the rules and requirements enacted to protect shareholders of public companies will be applied to your organization as well.

However, if your organization needs an audit that focuses on internal controls, operational effectiveness, and efficiency, or on ways to reduce risk, this audit can be performed by qualified people within the organization (called an internal audit). Certainly, a local CPA firm can provide this same type of review, but an internal audit can be performed by volunteers in the organization, resulting in a significant cost savings.

Some larger companies have an internal audit staff, whose function is to provide independent assurance and consulting services designed to improve an organization's operations. They can assist an organization in accomplishing its stated mission by evaluating the effectiveness of the organization's risk management, control, and governance process. The internal auditors also help detect and prevent fraud and ensure accurate financial reporting.

While a church may not have a dedicated internal auditor on their staff, they probably have access to qualified businessmen and -women in their congregation who are knowledgeable about corporate governance, accounting practices, and risk management.

If a financial statement audit isn't what your organization needs, a team of qualified people could be tasked to review your financial processes. Their objective would be to assess:

- The reliability and integrity of your financial information
- Compliance with internal policies and other laws and regulations
- Effectiveness and efficiency of operations

These types of reviews will address any errors that significantly impact the organization's ability to meet their stated goals and objectives.

audit options: which one is right for you?

Review the following table to determine which type of audit is right for your organization.

External Audit	
Process	Review of accounting practices and comparison to GAAP
Focus	Externally prepared financial statements that will be materially accurate
Benefit	Confidence in your accounting process and financial reporting
Internal Audit	
Process	Review of financial operations and internal controls for strengths and weaknesses
Focus	Testing the accuracy of internally-generated financial statements
Benefit	Confidence in your financial management process

embracing accountability and integrity

One of the most important steps leaders can take to prevent fraud from occurring in their church is to embrace accountability and integrity, and decide these are nonnegotiable values in the church. This means practicing what you preach and modeling biblical stewardship.

While you and your leadership are modeling these nonnegotiable values, weave these themes in your preaching and teaching. Teach on stewardship regularly and the importance of accountability and integrity in personal finances as well as corporate finance. Be transparent by providing regular financial reports.

The Evangelical Council for Financial Accountability is an organization dedicated to improving the public's trust in Christian ministries. They have established the "Seven Standards of Responsible Stewardship" which focus on board governance, financial transparency, integrity in fundraising, and proper use of charity resources.[41]

I would encourage your ministry to review and adopt these stewardship standards to demonstrate your commitment to biblical stewardship and financial accountability. For more information about the ECFA and their stewardship standards, visit their website at http://www.ECFA.org.

ECFA's Seven Standards of Responsible Stewardship

Standard 1 - Doctrinal Issues: Every organization shall subscribe to a written statement of faith clearly affirming a commitment to the evangelical Christian faith or shall otherwise demonstrate such commitment and shall operate in accordance with biblical truths and practices.

Standard 2 - Governance: Every organization shall be governed by a responsible board of not less than five individuals, a majority of whom shall be independent, who shall meet at least semiannually to establish policy and review its accomplishments.

Standard 3 - Financial Oversight: Each organization shall prepare complete and accurate financial statements. The board or a committee consisting of a majority of independent members shall approve the engagement of an independent certified public accountant, review the annual financial statements and maintain appropriate communication with the independent certified public accountant. The board shall be apprised of any material weaknesses in internal control or other significant risks.

Standard 4 - Use of Resources and Compliance with Laws: Every organization shall exercise the appropriate management and controls necessary to provide reasonable assurance that all of the organization's operations are carried out and resources are used in a responsible manner and in conformity with applicable laws and regulations, such conformity taking into account biblical mandates.

Standard 5 - Transparency: Every organization shall provide a copy of its current financial statements upon written request and shall provide other disclosures as the law may require. The financial statements required to comply with Standard 3 must be disclosed under this standard.

An organization must provide a report, upon written request, including financial information on any specific project for which it has sought or is seeking gifts.

Standard 6 – Compensation and Related Party Transactions: Every organization shall set compensation of its top leader and address related-party transactions in a manner that demonstrates integrity and propriety in conformity with ECFA's Policy for Excellence in Compensation-Setting and Related-Party Transactions.

Standard 7 - Stewardship of Charitable Gifts:

7.1 Truthfulness in Communications: In securing charitable gifts, all representations of fact, descriptions of the financial condition of the organization, or narratives about events must be current, complete, and accurate. References to past activities or events must be appropriately dated. There must be no material omissions or exaggerations of fact, use of misleading photographs or any other communication which would tend to create a false impression or misunderstanding.

7.2 Giver Expectations and Intent: Statements made about the use of gifts by an organization in its charitable gift appeals must be honored. A giver's intent relates both to what was communicated in the appeal and to any instructions accompanying the gift, if accepted by the organization. Appeals for charitable gifts must not create unrealistic expectations of what a gift will actually accomplish.

7.3 Charitable Gift Communication: Every organization shall provide givers appropriate and timely gift acknowledgments.

7.4 Acting in the Best Interest of Givers: When dealing with persons regarding commitments on major gifts, an organization's representatives must seek to guide and advise givers to adequately consider their broad interests.

An organization must make every effort to avoid knowingly accepting a gift from or entering into a contract with a giver that would place a hardship on the giver or place the giver's future well-being in jeopardy.

7.5 ***Percentage Compensation for Securing Charitable Gifts:*** An organization may not base compensation of outside stewardship resource consultants or its own employees directly or indirectly on a percentage of charitable contributions raised.

If you experience fraud

at your organization,

the actions you take will

directly impact the risk

of future frauds occurring.

SECTION TWO

Case Studies

TRUE STORIES OF

FRAUD & PRACTICAL

WAYS TO PREVENT IT

SKIMMING DONATIONS

The director had finished unpacking the last moving box when the bookkeeper walked into his office. "I have a confession," she said quietly. The director sat down and listened as the bookkeeper confessed to skimming donations received through the ministry's mail.

The director had been selected recently to lead the ministry that was dedicated to helping orphans, foster kids, and teenage mothers. He had introduced himself to each staff member and scheduled his first staff meeting. The bookkeeper's sudden confession surprised him, but it also puzzled him. *Why confess now?* he thought to himself. He soon had his answer. The bookkeeper stated that she didn't want to continue her deceit any longer. She wanted the organization and the new director to succeed and offered her resignation.

She went on to explain how she committed her abuse. The organization often solicited donations in the forms of cash and gift cards. Both were used to provide personal items for the children that the ministry supported.

She explained that whenever the secretary received cash in the mail, the cash was counted by two people and recorded in a log. The cash and a copy of the log were provided to the bookkeeper who made the deposit and recorded the contribution.

Any gift cards received in the mail, however, were given directly to the bookkeeper. The team members who counted the cash did not count or make a record of the gift cards received.

The bookkeeper maintained a log of the gift cards, but she didn't list each gift card individually, only a total of the gift cards by vendor. For example, if five Wal-Mart gift cards for $20 were received in May, she would list that as "$100 to Wal-Mart" in her spreadsheet.

When the bookkeeper received an approved purchase request, she would determine if there was an appropriate gift card that could be used for the purchase. If so, she would give the gift card to the staff member who would make the purchase and then return the gift card with the receipt. The bookkeeper would log the purchase in her spreadsheet and code it to the correct expense account. She tried to mark the remaining balance on each gift card, but that didn't always happen.

At the end of each month, she would forward the gift card spreadsheets to the local accounting firm who would record the total gift cards received as revenue (donation in kind) and post the gift card usage to the correct expense accounts.

The bookkeeper admitted that she didn't always record all the gift cards in her spreadsheets. At various times over the years, she would take various gift cards and use them to make personal purchases, but she wasn't sure how much she had taken over the years.

The ministry director suspended the bookkeeper and immediately began an investigation.

According to the financial records, the organization received between $14,000 and $16,000 in donated gift cards each year. In the past five years, the organization received about $76,800. During the same period, the bookkeeper had recorded that $69,500 in gift cards had been used to support children associated with the ministry.

Unfortunately, an audit revealed that there was no way to verify the accuracy of the bookkeeper's spreadsheets. It was apparent some records were incomplete or missing. Therefore, the auditor couldn't substantiate the total amount of gift cards received and used. This also made it difficult to determine how many gift cards were taken from the ministry and converted for personal use.

The auditor found 462 gift cards throughout the bookkeeper's office. They were not locked up or secured in any container. Some were in her desk drawer, some were on top of the desk, some were in a box on her credenza, and some were inside her credenza. The gift cards ranged from six cents to $100 each. There were approximately 25 different vendors representing clothing stores, grocery stores, bookstores, electronics showrooms, office suppliers, as well as prepaid Visa cards.

Although the auditor expected that these gift cards would total an unused value of $7,300 (gift cards received less gift cards used), the organization would have to call the vendor on all 462 gift cards to know for sure.

Unfortunately, too many weaknesses existed within this organization to determine the total value of gift cards misused, whether other employees were involved, and whether the value of gift cards received and used were accurately reported on the organization's financial records.

After the investigation, the employee was fired, but did offer to make restitution of a specified amount in lieu of prosecution.

what went wrong

In this case study, abuse occurred because there was a lack of accountability over gift cards received in the mail. Unfortunately, the person who opened the mail just delivered the gift cards to the bookkeeper without documenting the amounts received. Only the bookkeeper was in charge of recording when gift cards were received, and when gift cards were used. A second person was not made responsible for reconciling the gift card usage and ensuring the amounts recorded in the financial records were accurate.

Additionally, poor controls existed over the custody of the gift cards. The gift cards were not stored in a secure cabinet. Not only did the bookkeeper have unrestricted access to the gift cards, other employees could have walked into the office and taken gift cards for their own personal use, too.

Further, the ministry did not send contribution receipts to donors for their gift card donations—meaning significant contributions were not acknowledged by the ministry. If receipts or acknowledgment letters had been sent, a second person could have used those letters to verify the accuracy of the gift card logs.

best practices

Churches and other ministries currently receive most of their income through cash donations. Donations of cash and checks are collected during worship services or mailed to the church office.

While cash donations are more frequent, gift cards can be a convenient way for donors to make contributions to certain ministries. However, gift cards are easily convertible to cash and must be safeguarded just like cash.

Skimming is a type of fraud scheme where cash is stolen from an organization before it can be recorded in the financial records. If proper controls are not in place, skimming is a fraud risk that all churches face. Cash can be skimmed from the offering plate, from the mail, from the bookstore, or from the coffee shop—anywhere a church may receive cash.

Skimming is one of the more frequent ways funds are stolen from an organization, but can be difficult to identify. According to the ACFE study, skimming occurred in 14.6 percent of fraud cases reviewed and the scheme often lasted twenty-four months before being discovered.[42]

For this reason, churches need to have strong controls over cash receipts and donations. For example, all cash and gift card donations must be received, counted, and logged by at least two people. The gift card logs should reflect the original amount of the donation and any activity. The remaining balances on the gift cards should be reconciled by someone other than the custodian of the gift cards, and the gift cards must be stored in a secure cabinet or container.

Further, contribution receipts should be sent to the donors to acknowledge their gift. This process will also provide secondary accountability by helping to find any discrepancies between the actual and reported gift card amounts.

evaluate your organization

- ❏ Are all incoming cash and gift cards received, counted, and logged by at least two people? Who are they? What functions do they perform?
- ❏ Are cash and gift cards properly safeguarded while in your custody? Where are they stored? Who has access? How secure is the actual storage location?
- ❏ Is gift card usage reported accurately in the financial records?

❑ Are receipts sent to donors for gift card contributions and copies maintained in the files?

❑ Are gift card logs (received and used) reconciled by someone other than the gift card custodian? Who performs the reconciliation? How often? How are differences resolved?

for further review

If you would like to assess the strength of your financial controls in this area, perform a mini-audit by following these steps:

1. Review the process to receive, open, and record donations received through the mail.
2. Determine if the donations are accountable throughout the entire process by determining the following:
   a. Are cash and checks handled by at least two people while being received, counted, posted to the financial records, and deposited in the bank?
   b. Are gift cards handled by at least two people while being received, counted, and posted to the financial records or logs?
   c. Are gift cards kept in a locked container until used?
   d. Are gift card activities maintained in a log with current balances?
   e. Is gift card usage recorded in the financial records?
   f. Are gift card balances reconciled regularly by someone other than the gift card custodian?

3. Review the accuracy of the gift card logs. Select ten to twenty gift cards to test. Verify the remaining balance of each gift card with the provider, and match each balance on the gift card log.

4. Review the recording of gift card usage. Trace any purchases made with the gift cards selected in step 3 to the financial records.

If proper controls

are not in place,

skimming is a fraud risk

that all churches face.

SECRET BANK ACCOUNT

During the monthly meeting to review the ministry's financial operations, the bookkeeper went through the details of revenue and expenses, upcoming bills, and available cash. The ministry director was particularly interested in the funds collected to help open a campus ministry in the area. The bookkeeper reminded him that all funds collected were deposited into a separate bank account segregated from other ministry funds. She stated that although the campus ministry had recently opened, some funds remained left to be disbursed. After paying a few outstanding invoices, the campus ministry fund would be depleted.

The ministry director was satisfied with the information and directed the bookkeeper to pay the remaining bills and then close the campus ministry bank account.

The bookkeeper paid the remaining bills but kept the bank account open until the final few checks had cleared the account. During the next monthly meeting, the bookkeeper stated that the final bills were paid, and the bank account would be closed soon, as a few checks still had not cleared the bank. She explained it would take another month for the final checks to process through the account. The ministry director smiled and crossed the item off the agenda. "I guess we can remove this from the agenda," he stated. And with the strike of a pen, the topic of the campus ministry bank account was never revisited.

Unfortunately, the bookkeeper didn't close the campus ministry bank account, soon realizing that she was the only one who knew the account was still open. Since she was the person who opened the mail, including the bank statements, she was able to conceal the fact that the account was still open.

The bookkeeper began transferring money from the operating fund to the campus ministry fund. She started small—transferring only a few hundred dollars, disguising the transfer in the financial records as a routine expense.

Even though she was confident that no one would notice the transfer, she waited. As the organization's bookkeeper, she was an authorized signer on the bank accounts, which allowed her to write checks, make transfers, and withdraw funds. No one, not even the ministry director, looked at the financial records in detail, choosing only to see summary reports.

After a few weeks passed, no one asked about the transfer, so the bookkeeper went to the bank and withdrew the money. The next month, the bookkeeper decided it was time for another transfer. Only this time, the transfer was a little larger. Again, she concealed the transfer as a routine expense, and she went to the bank and made a withdrawal. Over the next year, she continued to make large transfers from the operating fund into the campus ministry fund. After each transfer, she went to the bank and withdrew all the funds.

Fortunately, while no one at the nonprofit noticed the embezzlement, someone at the bank was taking notice. The alert bank employee began noticing a pattern—after each transfer into the account, the bookkeeper would withdraw all the funds. The suspicious pattern caused the bank manager to contact the ministry director.

By the time the ministry director learned about the scheme, the bookkeeper had embezzled more than $57,600 over two years.

After a short investigation, the bookkeeper was terminated and agreed to make restitution in lieu of criminal prosecution.

what went wrong

In this case study, the bookkeeper was entrusted to close an unneeded bank account. Certainly, most employees in our churches and ministries are trustworthy. However, abuse can occur when a lack of accountability exists. In this case study, no one followed up to make sure the bookkeeper actually closed the account.

As a result, the bookkeeper was able to keep the second bank account hidden, transfer funds into the secret account, and use the funds for personal use.

Several internal control weaknesses allowed this abuse to occur, including:

- The organization's management failed to review the bookkeeper's actions to ensure the bank account was closed.
- The bookkeeper had signature authority for all bank accounts and the ability to transfer funds without additional approval.
- The bookkeeper received all the mail, including the bank statements.

As a result of these weaknesses, the bookkeeper had complete control over the financial records. This allowed the bookkeeper to disguise her transactions, manipulate reports and conceal her fraudulent activity.

best practices

Segregation of duties is an important internal control. No one employee should have unrestricted and unaccountable control over the finances. In many churches and ministries, the accounting function is limited to one or two people. As a result, one person usually has total control over the finances. However, additional measures can be added to provide accountability and oversight.

As noted earlier, the survey completed by KPMG in 2011 found 74 percent of fraudsters were able to perpetrate their crimes by exploiting weak internal controls.[43] This was a significant increase from their 2007 study that found only 49 percent of fraud cases occurred by exploiting weak controls.[44]

A lack of accountability is a common weakness in non-profit organizations, which can lead to significant abuse. For example, in August 2013, the CEO of a non-profit charter school in Philadelphia pled guilty to stealing $88,000. Through bank accounts that only he controlled, the CEO withdrew funds from the school and a sister organization with which he used to purchase a house for himself. He concealed his activity by disguising the withdrawals as legitimate labor expenses.[45]

While industry experts and best practices encourage accountability and strong controls, this continues to be the weak link in the financial processes at many churches and non-profits.

In order to keep all bank activity accountable and transparent in your organization, consider implementing these controls:

- Limit signature authority on bank accounts to those who are needed to transact business.
- Separate the functions of writing checks and reconciling bank activity.
- The person who reconciles the bank account should receive all the bank statements.
- All checks, electronic funds transfers, withdrawals, and wire transfers should require proper approval before the transaction occurs.

evaluate your organization

❑ Do you limit signature authority on bank accounts to those who are needed to transact business? Who currently has signature authority? What functions do they perform?

❑ Do you separate the functions of writing checks from the bank reconciliation activity? Who performs each of these functions?

❑ Do all bank statements go directly to the person who reconciles the bank account? Are there any exceptions to this process? How often and why?

❑ Do all checks, electronic funds transfers, withdrawals, and wire transfers require proper approval before the transaction occurs? What is the approval process and who is involved?

for further review

If you would like to assess the strength of your financial controls in this area, perform a mini-audit by following these steps:

1. Determine who has authority to sign checks. Evaluate whether these people have the ability to enter transactions into the general ledger.
2. Determine if the person who reconciles the bank statements is authorized to sign checks.
3. Verify that bank reconciliations are performed timely and completely.
4. Review bank statement activity for three to six months.
   a. Review activity for reasonableness.
   b. Verify that all withdrawals and electronic funds transfers were appropriate, properly approved, and posted to the general ledger.
5. Review canceled checks and determine the appropriateness of any checks written for cash or deposited into other bank accounts.

WRITING BLANK CHECKS

The president of the organization sat at his desk stunned. An independent auditor had just walked into his office and revealed that a trusted employee was probably stealing funds from the ministry. Even more disturbing was that the theft had been occurring for at least eighteen months. Several questions raced through the president's mind: "Is this true?" "How could this happen?" "Why didn't we catch this earlier?" "How are we going to move forward?"

ABC Publishing[46] was a ministry organization that printed religious materials, training resources, and Bibles in various languages. Their staff included missionaries, editors, and translators. Many staff and department leaders often traveled overseas to track the progress of their ongoing projects, often leaving a few administrative and support staff alone in the office.

The office manager was assigned the task of overseeing much of the office's administrative duties including purchasing office supplies, office decor, and hospitality items.

When the office manager needed to make a purchase, she would submit a purchase request to the vice-president for approval. Upon approval, the chief financial officer would write a check and have an authorized person sign the check. Only the president, vice-president, and chief financial officer (CFO) were authorized to sign checks. If an invoice wasn't attached to the purchase request, the CFO asked the office manager to return the check stub with an invoice or receipt once the purchase was made.

Often, the exact total of the purchase wasn't known when the purchase request was submitted. The vendor's name and a description of the items being purchased were on the request, but not a total dollar amount. The organizational leadership agreed to sign a blank check as long as the office manager turned in a receipt afterwards.

The first time the office manager requested a blank check to purchase office supplies, the CFO requested she bring back the check stub and receipt. After making the purchase, she carefully folded the receipt so the purchase total was clearly visible and stapled it to the check stub. When she returned the check stub to the CFO, he asked her two questions: "Did the vice-president approve this purchase?" and "Did you attach the receipt to the check stub?" The office manager answered yes to both questions, knowing that the exchange was just a formality since the CFO had the vice-president sign the blank check, and he could see that the receipt was attached to the check stub.

The office manager watched as the CFO went to his computer, opened the financial software program, entered the check into the financial records, and placed the check stub in the filing cabinet with paperwork for other completed transactions.

She walked away and thought, "That worked well." Over the next few weeks, she requested a couple more blank checks. After a while, she realized that while the CFO would always ask "Did the vice-president approve this purchase?" and "Did you attach the receipt to the check stub?" he never actually looked at the receipt. Further, the vice-president never asked to review the receipt before she returned it to the CFO. The office manager appreciated the fact that the organization's leadership viewed her as a trusted employee, but she also realized she had more freedom than she thought.

The president shook his head in disbelief and asked the auditor to explain what had happened. As far as the auditor could tell, at some point, the office manager realized that even though she turned in a receipt for every blank check, no one actually reviewed the receipt to make sure the items purchased were business-related. While the auditor didn't know the reason behind her actions, it was evident that she soon realized she could make personal purchases and use ministry funds to pay for it.

When the auditor reviewed the receipts as part of his normal testing, he discovered that gift cards were included in many of these transactions that started with a blank check. The gift cards, which could be purchased near the check-out lane, were clearly identified on the receipts and included restaurant, grocery, and retail establishments. As he looked through the financial files, he determined that these gift card purchases had started approximately eighteen months earlier. At first, the gift card amounts were low, but over time, the auditor noticed that the gift card amounts increased. He also noticed that several gift cards were purchased at a time— each one clearly itemized on the receipt.

The auditor noticed that while the office manager had turned in the receipts, she was clearly trying to hide her activity. In fact, she purposely folded the receipt and stapled it in such a way to hide the items being purchased. Someone would have to remove the staple and unfold the receipt in order to view the list of purchased items.

The organization's president confirmed to the auditor that his organization didn't use or give away gift cards. These gift cards were definitely unapproved purchases. The president confronted the employee and suspended her. The case was then turned over to legal counsel for further review and investigation.

By the time the auditor uncovered the theft, the office manager had purchased $9,000 in gift cards, ranging in amounts from $25 to $300.

what went wrong

In this case study, the office manager was a very talented and trusted employee. Due to her length of time at the organization, her passion for the ministry, and her accomplishments in the past, she had the trust and confidence of her supervisors. As a result, her supervisors didn't give a second thought to handing her a blank check.

While the CFO provided a measure of accountability by writing the vendor's name on the check, the office manager's only required task was to write the amount on the check at the store checkout. However, she abused her supervisor's trust by adding personal items to the purchase and using ministry funds for payment.

Several internal control weaknesses allowed this abuse to occur, which included:

- The office manager submitted her purchase for preapproval, but no manager reviewed her purchases afterward.
- The vice-president frequently signed blank checks for the office manager's use.
- The office manager's purchases were not reviewed to determine if the items purchased complied with internal policies.
- The president, vice-president, and CFO all failed to hold the office manager accountable for her purchases.

As a result of misplaced trust, this fraud scheme continued for over eighteen months before being discovered.

best practices

Writing blank checks is a fast and convenient way to allow employees to make purchases. However, signed, blank checks can be easily abused. Not only can the checks be written for more than the approved amounts, the checks can be used for entirely different purchases.

Issuing unauthorized checks or "check tampering" is a common fraud scheme. For example, in April 2013, an office manager was sentenced to almost three years in prison for embezzling more than $900,000 from her employer using this scheme. She was able to convince the check signers at the company to sign blank checks under the assumption that they would be used to pay company expenses. Instead, she cashed the checks and used the money for her own personal benefit. Once the blank checks were signed, she tried to conceal the fraud and implicate someone else by making the checks out to another employee and then forging the employee's endorsement on the back of the check. Besides the fraud, she was also convicted of identity theft.[47]

One recent fraud study found issuing or forging unauthorized company checks was the most common embezzlement scheme.[48] Another study found that check tampering was the second most common fraud scheme perpetrated on religious and charitable organizations.[49] Unfortunately, the median duration of check tampering schemes lasted around thirty months before being discovered at these religious and charitable organizations.

Don't let this happen at your organization. When writing checks, there are several steps a church can take to keep fraud from occurring. These controls include:

- Maintaining a policy to never sign blank checks
- Securing blank check stock in a locked cabinet
- Keeping track of check numbers used and reconciling check numbers to remaining blank check stock
- Matching supporting documents to each check's amount before signing checks
- Requiring supporting documents to be original invoices or receipts—not copies, partial documents or estimates
- Using purchase requests or requisition forms to authorize purchases before they occur
- Reviewing itemized receipts or invoices for appropriateness and compliance with the organization's policies

evaluate your organization

- ❑ Do you make it a practice to never sign blank checks? Do exceptions occur? Why?
- ❑ Do you secure blank check stock in a locking cabinet? Who has access to the locking cabinet?
- ❑ Do you keep track of pre-numbered check stock and reconcile unused check numbers to the checks already printed? Who performs this reconciliation? How often?
- ❑ Do you review supporting documents and match amounts to the checks before signing? Who performs

this review? What happens if supporting documents aren't available?

❏ Do you require original invoices and receipts for payment? What happens if original documents aren't available?

❏ Do you require properly approved purchase requests or requisition forms before purchases are made? What is the process to get approval? Who has authority to approve purchases?

❏ Do you review the itemized receipts or invoices for appropriateness and compliance with the organization's policies? Who performs this review? What happens if a purchase doesn't comply with policy?

for further review

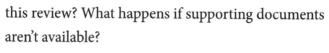ould you like to know if your controls are strong enough to prevent this from happening at your ministry? Perform a mini-audit of how you write checks by following these steps:

1. Interview the bookkeeping staff to determine if blank checks are commonly used.
2. Obtain a list of all checks written within the past three months. Pick a sample of twenty-five checks to review.
   a. Obtain canceled checks. (Your bank may provide copies of the check with the monthly bank statement.)

b. Determine if purchases were properly approved.

c. Match the canceled checks to the supporting receipts or invoices.

d. Review the itemized receipts to determine if the purchases were appropriate and complied with the organization's policies.

3. Consider changes to policy or process to strengthen this area if any weaknesses exist.

Writing blank checks

is fast and convenient;

however, blank checks

can be easily abused.

CHARGE ACCOUNTS

The church bookkeeper ended the conversation by stating, "I'll be right there," and hung up the phone. His wife could see the look of disbelief on his face and asked him what was going on. "That was the police," he began. "They just arrested the hospitality coordinator. I have to go to the police station."

Main Street Church had been in the community for over fifty years. Family members of the founding group that started the congregation still attended each week. The church had grown large enough that they needed a person to oversee the hospitality ministry. This person was assigned to manage the kitchen, order supplies and food, and organize the meals for special dinners, funerals or church functions.

In order to facilitate her purchasing requests, the church opened up a revolving charge account with a local supermarket. The supermarket provided personalized cards that would allow the bearer to charge the purchase to the church. The church provided these cards to several people, including the hospitality coordinator.

Each month, the supermarket would send a bill to the church with a summary of the charges. In order to properly code the expenses, the bookkeeper requested each person who used the supermarket charge card to turn in the receipts. At the end of the month, the bookkeeper would match the receipts to the monthly bill, allocate the purchases to the appropriate expense account, and pay the bill.

Unfortunately, the bookkeeper realized that several receipts were missing each month. He was obligated to pay the bill, but he didn't know how to allocate several purchases each month. He was also unsure of whether it was an appropriate purchase, or if the supermarket had charged the church's account improperly.

The bookkeeper met with each person who had a supermarket charge card and reminded them that they must turn in the receipts each time they use the card. He showed them the few purchases each month that were unaccounted for. Unfortunately, each person denied making the mysterious purchases.

The bookkeeper considered keeping the charge cards locked up and under the supervision of the office manager. The office manager could hand out the cards when needed, and retrieve them after the purchase was completed. When the card was returned, she could make sure that the receipt was turned in with it. However, this additional control was met with resistance from church leaders. The office manager worked part time, and none of the employees wanted to be restricted to shopping only when the office manager was working.

The bookkeeper had two more months go by without any improvement in the number of receipts being turned in. He realized if he couldn't get his staff's support, maybe he could get the supermarket's support. He met with the supermarket's accounting department who agreed to send copies of the receipts with each month's bill. At last, the bookkeeper would have a matching receipt and be able to allocate the expenses to the appropriate department.

When he opened up the next month's bill, the bookkeeper was shocked at what he saw. All the receipts were included, but he didn't expect to see some of the items that were purchased. Included with some of the purchases were several supermarket gift cards. These gift cards, which could only be used at this supermarket, ranged in value from $50 to $200.

He considered that these may have been purchased to give to a needy family, but a quick conversation with the pastor revealed that wasn't the case.

He wondered if this may have been the reason that past receipts hadn't been turned it. He contacted the supermarket manager who was able to provide receipts for the previous twelve months. As he feared, the receipts that had been missing all included gift cards in the purchase.

The bookkeeper still didn't know who was doing this, so he interviewed the staff one more time with the new information. Again, each person denied making the purchases that included the gift cards.

The bookkeeper asked for the supermarket's help again. He asked them to require signatures when the charge card was used. When the next month's bill arrived, there were signatures on each receipt. However, he was shocked to see several receipts still included gift cards—and flabbergasted to see the name of the pastor's wife scrawled on the bottom of those receipts.

Fortunately, the bookkeeper had known the pastor's wife long enough to recognize her signature—and this was clearly a forgery. Someone had been stealing from the church, and now they were willing to implicate the pastor's wife.

The bookkeeper visited with the supermarket management team one more time. Along with the questionable receipts, he carried the most recent pictorial directory of the church. Each staff member who had used a church charge card had their picture in this directory.

The supermarket's management team was clearly concerned. Not only did the church have poor controls over their purchasing process, the supermarket had some poor controls too. The supermarket staff had allowed someone to fraudulently charge purchases to the church.

Thankfully, the receipts listed the ID of the cashier and time of day. Management talked with the cashier who recalled the most recent transaction. They asked her to look through the directory and pick out the church member who came through her line that day. It didn't take her long to find the picture. She pointed to the picture of the hospitality coordinator and exclaimed, "That's her!"

Incredibly, the hospitality coordinator went back to the supermarket to make another purchase. But this time, the supermarket staff was on the lookout. As soon as she entered the store, they called the police. Before she could check out, she was arrested.

By the time the scheme was discovered, the bookkeeper estimated the hospitality coordinator had purchased over $4,000 in personal items and shopping cards.

what went wrong

In this case study, the church's charge account at a local supermarket was abused by a trusted leader in the church. Unfortunately, trust is not an effective internal control. Several weaknesses allowed this abuse to occur, including:

- Staff members were allowed to charge purchases to the church account without any preapproval.
- There wasn't an effective process to make sure staff members turned in receipts after a purchase was charged to the church account.

- There was a lack of accountability to ensure that purchases were appropriate and complied with the church's policies.

Not only did the church have poor procedures, but so did the supermarket. The supermarket was complicit in this scheme because they allowed people to charge purchases to the church account without verifying who they were.

best practices

Having a charge account at a local supermarket or wholesale food store is a convenient way to make purchases. Several employees can be authorized to make purchases for the church, the employees don't have to request a church check for the purchase, and the church only receives one bill at the end of the month.

However, these benefits are also the reason charge accounts can be abused. Employees can make purchases without first obtaining authorization, employees can bypass any accountability measures by not turning in receipts, and churches can lose visibility of purchase totals until the monthly bill arrives.

In order to keep charge account purchases accountable, consider implementing these controls:

- Restrict access to charge accounts to as few employees as possible.
- Use purchase request forms to authorize any charge account activity before it occurs.

- Request the store to require proper identification and signatures for each charge purchase.
- Require employees to turn in receipts after each purchase.
- Reconcile receipts to the monthly bill.
- Review itemized receipts for appropriateness and compliance with the organization's policies.

As an additional measure of control, consider keeping the charge cards locked up. The charge card could be handed out once the purchase is authorized and the purchaser would be required to return the receipt with the card once the purchase has been completed.

evaluate your organization

- ❑ Do you restrict access to charge accounts to only those employees who have a valid need? Who are those employees? What functions do they perform?
- ❑ Do you use purchase request forms to authorize any charge account activity before it occurs? Who authorizes purchases on charge accounts?
- ❑ Do you require the store to check for proper identification and obtain a signature for each charge purchase?
- ❑ Do you require employees to turn in receipts after each purchase? What happens if receipts are not turned in?
- ❑ Do you reconcile receipts to the monthly bill? What happens if discrepancies are noted?

❑ Do you review the itemized receipts for appropriateness and compliance with the organization's policies? What happens if a purchase doesn't comply with policy?

❑ Do you have an adequate process to keep track of the charge cards and obtain all receipts? Is there anything you can do to strengthen the process?

for further review

If you would like to assess the strength of your financial controls in the area of revolving credit and charge accounts, perform a mini-audit by following these steps:

1. Obtain a list of employees who have access to charge accounts and validate their need for a card. Perform this review annually.
2. Review invoices for three months.
   a. Determine if all receipts were turned in and attached to monthly invoice.
   b. Determine if preapproval was obtained and documented for each charge.
   c. Review itemized list of items purchased to determine if they were appropriate and complied with church policy.
3. If any weaknesses exist, consider changes to policy or process to strengthen this area.

SEPARATE CHECKING ACCOUNTS

The board member's question made the senior pastor pause for a moment. As he reflected on the question, he wasn't sure why the youth pastor had a checking account separate from the church's main checking account.

He remembered it was that way when he became senior pastor fifteen years earlier. Although this current youth pastor had only been here for a few years, the senior pastor allowed the separate finances to continue. *If it worked before, why change it?* he remembered thinking.

He quickly thought through the process. The youth pastor set his own budget each year, raised his own funds, purchased any ministry items and supplies, and reported on his ministry's financial operations each year at the annual business meeting.

While the youth minster's salary and benefits were paid through the church's general fund, most everything else related to the youth ministry was run through the youth checking account. At times, the church board would transfer funds to the youth ministry for a special project or need, but it was only occasionally.

But now, some of the board member's concerns seemed to make sense. Any offerings collected during the youth service were handled by the youth pastor or his youth workers. The senior pastor assumed the youth had good procedures to count the offerings, but he couldn't be sure. Further, he didn't know how youth funds were actually spent, or what they were spent on, other than the summary report he saw once a year with everyone else at the annual business meeting. He thought the youth pastor mentioned that he used financial software to help manage the ministry finances, but he wasn't sure which one.

After discussing the potential risks that could occur when one person has complete control over contributions, disbursements and reporting, he agreed that it was appropriate to have the youth ministry fund combined with the rest of the church's finances.

The two also discussed that this decision would involve several changes. Two ushers would have to collect the youth offering and place it in the church safe so that it could be counted with the other church offerings. The youth's income and expense activity for the current year would have to be combined with all the other church financial activity so that monthly and annual reports would be complete. The youth minister would no longer have authority to write checks. The youth checking account would need to be closed and any remaining funds would be transferred to the church's main checking account. The youth minister would have to submit check requests for review and approval, and all checks would have to be signed by two board members.

While the change could be overwhelming to the youth minister, the senior pastor realized it would bring all ministry leaders in the church under the same financial process and accountability.

The pastor presented the idea to the board, who agreed with the decision. When the change was presented to the youth minister, he seemed to embrace the new process and accountability. Immediately, youth offerings were collected and counted with the main church offerings. The youth minister began submitting check requests for review and approval, and two board members signed the checks.

However, the youth minister didn't turn over his checkbook register, detailed financial reports for the past year, or even a backup of his financial software. At first, he needed time to enter recent activity into the financial software; then he needed time to reconcile the bank statements; then his hard drive got corrupted and he needed to reinstall all of his software and recreate data. Unfortunately, he said he didn't back up his financial data so he would have to reenter all the financial activity for the past year.

These excuses kept occurring for several months, which made the pastor and board suspicious. Since they weren't getting any cooperation from the youth minister, the pastor went to the bank for help. The bank provided bank statements and copies of all canceled checks for the past two years. When the pastor and treasurer reviewed the activity, they understood why the youth minister had been unwilling to provide his financial activity.

A review of the bank activity revealed that the youth minister was using ministry funds for expenses that were not allowed or appropriate. While no other staff member's spouse had a cell phone paid for by the church, the youth minister felt it was appropriate for his wife to have a cell phone paid with youth funds. While church policy allowed occasional business lunches, the youth minister used ministry funds to purchase frequent lunches. He also used ministry funds to purchase snack food and nutrition bars that he kept in his office. Further, the pastor noticed that when some of his requests for equipment purchases were not approved by the board, the youth minster used youth funds to make the purchase.

It was apparent that when the youth minister had the freedom to make his own purchase decisions, he frequently used ministry funds for purchases that were not appropriate or allowed under church policy.

what went wrong

I n this case study, a ministry leader was able to collect offerings, make deposits, and spend funds without submitting his activity for any other review or approval.

Several control weaknesses allowed this abuse to occur, including:

- The youth minister was allowed to have a separate checking account that was not included or rolled into the church's financial records.
- The youth minister's financial activity was not reviewed or approved by another ministry leader.
- The youth minister did not have a clear understanding of what expenses were appropriate for his ministry.

Additionally, the church did not have clear policies on how ministry funds should be managed. One of the easiest and most important controls a church can implement is the documentation of formal accounting policies and procedures, personnel policies and other operating policies.

best practices

M ost churches will have a small bookkeeping staff that oversees the financial processes. All transactions will run through this process, including contributions and expenses. However, some ministry leaders may see the centralized process as burdensome, stifling and restrictive. These ministry leaders may request to separate their ministry funds to streamline processes. This is how the youth minister in this case study was able to justify having a separate checking account.

However, the risks of having separate financial processes and bank accounts outweighed the benefits in this case. The youth minister was able to make purchases that were not accountable to anyone else, and abuse occurred.

In order to keep all financial activity accountable and transparent, consider implementing these controls:

- Require all offerings and contributions to follow the same collection, counting and deposit process.
- Do not allow ministry leaders to have separate bank accounts.
- Require all expenditures to follow the same request and approval process.
- Hold employees accountable by reviewing purchases for appropriateness and compliance with church policies.
- Prepare consolidated financial reports that include income and expenses for all departments.

Finally, remember that documented policies and procedures are an important component of strong internal controls. Written policies and procedures will provide accountability for staff members, define expectations, and minimize confusion.

evaluate your organization

❑ Do you require all offerings and contributions to follow the same collection, counting and deposit process? Are there any exceptions? Why?

❑ Do you allow ministry leaders to have separate bank accounts? Who are they? Why?

❑ Do you require all expenditures to follow the same request and approval process? Are there any exceptions? Why?

❑ Do you hold employees accountable by reviewing purchases for appropriateness and compliance with church policies? Who performs this review? What happens if a purchase doesn't comply with policy?

❑ Do you prepare consolidated financial reports that include income and expenses for all departments? If not, why? Are other reports available?

❑ Are your accounting policies and procedures, personnel policies, and other operating policies documented? Who has access to these documented policies? Have all appropriate personnel read and understood these documented policies?

for further review

If you would like to assess the strength of your financial controls in this area, perform a mini-audit by following these steps:

1. Review the collection of all offerings and contributions to determine if they all follow the same collection, counting and deposit process.

2. Obtain a list of all bank accounts used in the

organization and determine who has access and authorization to sign checks, make transfers, etc.

3. Review financial reports to ensure all ministry activity is included in the reports.

4. If any weaknesses exist, consider changes to policy or process to strengthen this area.

The easiest

and most important

control a church

can implement

is documentation of

policies and procedures.

ELECTRONIC FUNDS TRANSFERS

The interim pastor sat down at his desk, opened the mail and scanned the monthly statement for fuel charges. As the vendor intended, the bright red "past due" notice caught his eye. He had only been interim pastor for twenty days, but he didn't recognize this charge account. He was prepared to find a few bills that might have been overlooked during the transition, but as he reviewed the church's financial files, he didn't see any past activity for this particular company. "This must be a mistake," he thought to himself. He set the bill aside and made a mental note to have the secretary call the company and have them correct their mistake.

The next day, the pastor received another confusing bill in the mail. This time, the bill was from a local wholesale club and the balance due was significant. A quick scan of the monthly statement determined that a majority of the balance had been carried over from the previous month. Only a small payment had been made in the past thirty days to fulfill the minimum payment due. Because the total amount was not paid in full, substantial finance charges were accruing. "Is this another mistake?" he thought to himself.

The pastor was thoroughly concerned when he opened another envelope that contained a monthly installment bill for two desktop computers. He looked around the offices and noticed a new desktop in the bookkeeper's office, but he couldn't find a second one. He looked through the office files again, but didn't see any paperwork that showed the church had purchased any computers.

The pastor laid the paperwork down and considered the possibilities: Could all of these bills be a mistake, or was something else going on? He decided he needed help to figure this out.

The auditor arrived the next week and began reviewing the church's financial files, including the suspicious bills that the pastor had received. After interviewing current staff and reviewing financial reports, general ledger details, bank statements, canceled checks and other office files, the auditor had a clear understanding of the church's financial condition.

The pastor called a special board meeting and asked the auditor to join them. The auditor shared his findings with the board and revealed some disturbing news: The former pastor had used church funds for personal expenses and concealed this activity from the board and bookkeeper. The auditor proceeded to describe the depth and breadth of the abuse. The former pastor used church funds to make monthly payments on his personal charge accounts and credit cards. These payments were made through electronic funds transfers. Additionally, he had been using the church's charge accounts for his personal benefit.

To add insult to injury, the auditor explained that the abuse had significantly affected the church's cash flow. The abuse had become so rampant and encompassed so many accounts, that there weren't enough funds each month to pay for these fraudulent transactions, let alone the church's valid expenses. As a result, the former pastor had to resort to making minimum payments on many of these accounts because the church's weekly cash flow wasn't enough to pay the entire amounts. This exacerbated the problem since the church was accruing finance charges and late fees that added to the outstanding balances.

The board members were visibly stunned and wondered how this was concealed from them. The auditor explained that the pastor's access to the bank accounts allowed him to make several electronic funds transfers each month. He picked up the mail each day, which included the monthly bills, credit card statements, and bank statements. The pastor would tell the bookkeeper which checks to write and for how much. Neither the bookkeeper nor board members saw the actual bills or statements. Unfortunately, while the board received a summary financial report each month, it lacked sufficient details that would have allowed them to see this abuse.

The auditor explained that the pastor further concealed his activity by removing these monthly bills and statements from the church office. Support for many of the payments reflected on the church's bank statements could not be located in the church office. As a result, the auditor explained that the total amount of the abuse could not be calculated and suspected it was much larger. However, based on his review of the available documents, he determined the pastor's abuse consisted of:

- Using church funds to make electronic payments on three personal credit cards. The monthly payments ranged from $100 to $500 for at least two years.
- Spending up to $17,300 for personal items at a local wholesale club.
- Charging gasoline purchases to the church for family and friends—at least twenty-six purchases over a two-month period, and sometimes charging gas at multiple locations on the same day.
- Using church funds to pay for a computer that he gave to his wife.

- Having the church incur finance charges and late fees totaling $4,000.

The board discussed how the church would recover and move forward. They decided against taking legal action, but did provide the auditor's findings to the former pastor's ecclesiastical leadership. Unfortunately for the church, they had to make significant cutbacks in their planned spending over the next twelve months in order to pay off these outstanding balances.

what went wrong

In this case study, there was a lack of accountability and transparency in the church's financial operations. The former pastor was able to conceal his abuse of funds by having direct access to the bank account and bank statements. He also directed the bookkeeper to write checks, and directed board members to sign checks, without providing supporting documentation.

In the nonprofit world, trust is a much-desired character trait. I've often heard leaders say, "I give people my trust, until I have a reason not to." Certainly, this is a worthy attitude to have in our interpersonal relationships, but within the financial arena, trust is not an effective control.

This church did not have sufficient controls to ensure that disbursements were proper and adequately supported. The former pastor had online access to the bank accounts and would pay several bills electronically, without anyone knowing. The supporting invoices and monthly statements were not kept in the church office or provided to the board for review.

The former pastor would open the mail, pull out the bills, determine which ones should be paid, and give a list to the bookkeeper that contained the name of the vendor and the check amount. The bookkeeper would prepare the check, and a board member would sign the check and return it to the pastor for mailing. However, the person signing the check did not have the corresponding invoice to review when signing the check.

While the board received financial reports each month, they only received summary reports. They didn't have access to general ledger details that clearly identified all transactions. Without access to the invoices or general ledger details, many of the payments authorized by the former pastor (whether by check or electronic funds transfer) did not have an appropriate level of accountability and transparency.

best practices

Accountability and transparency are the key components of good stewardship. Because churches and nonprofits rely on donated funds to continue operations, it is crucial to have accountability and transparency for donor confidence. Accountability and transparency will also protect church leaders from accusations of impropriety or self-dealing.

More importantly, accountability and transparency can help prevent unauthorized wire transfers, which is a common way for embezzlement to occur. Consider the following cases:

- A Virginia woman pleaded guilty to embezzling nearly $570,000 from the American Diabetes Association. For over nine years, the treasury manager initiated 133 unauthorized wire transfers from the Association's bank account to a personal bank account that she controlled. To conceal her crime, she altered approved purchase request forms and accounting records to make the transfer look like legitimate expenses such as postage charges.[50]

- A grand jury indicted a forty-year old woman for allegedly embezzling more than $453,000 from her employer. For almost three years, the employee initiated electronic funds transfers from the company's bank account into her own bank account.[51]

To make sure that all payments, including electronic funds transfers, are accountable and transparent at your church, consider the following controls:

- When paying by check, the bookkeeper should prepare checks for payment and a board member or other authorized signer should sign checks only after reviewing supporting invoices.
- When paying by electronic funds transfer, the invoice should be reviewed and approved by a board member or other authorized signer before payment. The board member should initial the invoice and make a note that it would be paid via an electronic payment.
- Supporting documentation should be filed by vendor, with either the check stub attached to the invoice, or other notation that includes date paid and check number.

As an additional level of accountability, empower the bookkeeper and board members to ask for supporting documentation or additional details when preparing checks, signing checks, or recording the financial information. Further, a complete set of financial reports, including details of every transaction, should be provided to the governing board or the finance sub-committee each month.

evaluate your organization

- ❏ Do you require the treasurer or board members to review supporting documentation before signing checks? Do they know what documentation is appropriate? What happens if adequate documentation isn't available?
- ❏ Do you require proper approval before making payments by electronic funds transfer? Who has authority to approve transfers? How is approval documented?
- ❏ Do you keep check stubs and supporting documentation for accountability and transparency? How long is documentation maintained? Where is it stored?
- ❏ Do you empower check signers to request additional support, if needed, when approving disbursements?
- ❏ Do you provide a complete set of financial reports, including general ledger details, to the governing board each month?

for further review

If you would like to assess the strength of your financial controls in this area, perform a mini-audit by following these steps:

1. Review the bank statements for the previous six months.
2. Trace all withdrawals and electronic payments back to supporting documents. Verify proper approval and appropriateness.
3. Trace ten checks from each bank statement back to supporting documents. Verify proper approval and appropriateness.
4. Review the process to sign checks. Make sure checks are not signed without reviewing supporting documentation.

Accountability and transparency are the

key components of good stewardship.

CREDIT CARD ABUSE

The Chief Financial Officer (CFO) handed the business credit card to the new employee with a strict warning: "This is not a license to spend money indiscriminately. We have strict controls over the use of credit cards in our organization. This credit card is provided as a convenient way to make purchases, but those purchases must be approved in your departmental budget and you must turn in receipts for each and every transaction. We have additional requirements regarding use, approval, and documentation in our policy manual. I expect you to read it and comply."

Fortunately, the CFO required all employees to follow the established policies. When the monthly credit card statement was received, all employees were expected to attach receipts, identify the business purpose of the expense and note the appropriate account to charge the expense to. The Accounts Payable (AP) clerk was empowered to follow up with any employee who didn't follow the established procedures. That is, every employee except the CFO.

Over the years the AP clerk noticed that while all employees attached their receipts to the credit card statement, the CFO would place his receipts in an envelope and seal it before giving it to the clerk. The clerk was instructed to post all employees' expenses to the appropriate ledger and pay the monthly bill. However, the CFO stated that he would post the expenses for his own activity.

It seemed appropriate to her that the CFO would take an interest in the financials and post some of the activity. But now, as she scanned some of his activity, she became concerned. Many of the expenses didn't seem appropriate for their organization, and other employees didn't make similar purchases. She dismissed her concern by thinking, *Surely, the CFO would know what expenses were appropriate or not.* However, the charges continued for several months, and the CFO continued to submit his receipts in a sealed envelope. The AP clerk continued to file the envelope away and make the payments. While her suspicion was growing month after month, she continued to dismiss it.

As the AP clerk reviewed the current month's credit card bill, her heart sank. The CFO had made a purchase that was clearly not business related. Further, the transaction was not appropriate for an employee of this non-profit organization, let alone the CFO, who was also a minister. She knew it was time to let someone else know about her concerns.

As the AP clerk explained her concerns to the president of the organization, she showed him the CFO's credit card statement. The president confirmed that many of the transactions were not appropriate. He was surprised that the CFO sealed his receipts in an envelope while all others were expected to attach them to the statement; however, he admitted that he didn't require the CFO to submit his purchases for approval. Together, they reviewed the statements for the past twelve months. The president verified that multiple transactions each month were not appropriate, and decided it was time to confront the CFO.

Faced with the evidence presented, the CFO admitted that he used the organization's credit card for personal purchases and offered to make restitution. The president agreed and stated that he would request an audit to determine the total amount.

An audit revealed that during a four-year period, the CFO charged at least $20,000 in personal expenses to the organization. However, it was apparent that the abuse had been occurring longer. The abuse included purchases at local home improvement stores, frequent lunches near the office, frequent coffee and snacks around town, large purchases at clothing stores, extravagant meals while on travel, Starbucks gift certificates, golf items, and movie rentals at hotels.

The president terminated the CFO's employment and implemented new controls to keep this abuse from happening again.

what went wrong

In this case study, the CFO had established very strong controls at this ministry. The accounts receivable and accounts payable functions were performed by separate people. Disbursements were properly approved and adequately supported with invoices before a check was written and signed. The bank reconciliations were performed by someone who didn't sign checks. All employees were required to provide receipts for all credit card transactions, which the chief financial officer reviewed for appropriateness.

Unfortunately, no one reviewed the CFO's credit card transactions. No one held him accountable for his purchases. When he deviated from the established policies that everyone else had to follow, no one stopped him. While he was empowered to question purchases made by other staff members, no one was empowered to question his purchases.

This lack of accountability allowed his abuse to continue for more than four years. Although the accounts payable clerk noticed his deviation from established procedures, she finally had the courage to blow the whistle when she noticed suspicious transactions.

best practices

Credit cards are certainly a convenient way to make business purchases. They don't require any approval before use and are accepted all over the world. Unfortunately, these benefits contribute to their frequent abuse.

However, just like other expenditures, credit cards require adequate substantiation for all business expenses. Often times, though, it is hard to keep track of all those receipts—especially, if you are trying to conceal your activity.

Credit card statements must be supported with receipts. The credit card statement will reveal that a purchase was made, but in most cases, the item or service being purchased will not be very apparent. For example, the statement will reveal a purchase was made at a department store, but it will not describe the items purchased.

Further, in order to comply with IRS requirements for an accountable plan, actual receipts are required for credit card purchases. The business purpose will need to be identified. Further, for any meals or entertainment expenses, the names of those attending need to be identified.

Besides providing adequate support for every credit card transaction, it is necessary to have each transaction reviewed to determine if the purchase is an appropriate business expense. Without the itemized receipt, the appropriateness of the transaction cannot be determined. In this case study, while the CFO reviewed the appropriateness of purchases for other staff members, no one was reviewing his purchases for appropriateness.

This case study revealed one leader's activity was not transparent or accountable. To minimize this risk in your organization, foster a workplace environment where transparency is encouraged and accountability is welcomed. Create accountability measures between leadership and empower staff to hold each other accountable.

evaluate your organization

❑ Do you require receipts for all credit card transactions? What happens if receipts are not available?

❑ Do you note the business purpose of each transaction? Are staff members aware of what constitutes an acceptable business purpose for your organization?

❑ Do you identify the names of those attending meal and entertainment functions, as the IRS requires?

❑ Do you require secondary review and approval of all transactions? Who performs this approval? What happens if a transaction doesn't comply with policy?

❑ Do you foster a workplace environment that encourages transparency and accountability? Do all leaders promote an ethical climate throughout the organization?

for further review

If you would like to assess the strength of your financial controls in this area, perform a mini-audit by following these steps:

1. Pick three credit card statements to review.
   a. Determine if every transaction is supported by an appropriate receipt or invoice.
   b. Determine if the business purpose of each transaction is clearly identified.
   c. For meals and entertainment, determine if the names of those attending are clearly identified.
2. Determine if each expense was charged to the appropriate general ledger account.
3. Determine if credit card purchases are reviewed and approved by an appropriate supervisor.

While the CFO was empowered to

question the purchases made by

other staff members, no one was em-

powered to question his purchases.

CREDIT CARD REFUNDS

The accounts receivable manager walked into her office one morning and noticed the phone message lying on her desk. With a staff member home sick, she had come into the office early that morning to catch up on some work. She had a lot of work ahead of her if she was going to meet some pending deadlines.

The manager worked for a ministry organization that operated a bookstore where parishioners could purchase books, music, and Bible study materials. The manager and her staff were responsible for billing customers and processing credit card payments.

After reading the message, she decided to put aside the tasks she had planned to work on and spend some time researching this new matter. The phone message was from a customer who called to question why they had received a bill when they hadn't ordered any product.

Normally, the manger's accounting clerk would handle this issue, but he was at home recovering from the flu, so she decided to look into this customer's complaint.

The manager pulled a copy of the invoice and noticed that the customer hadn't purchased any product in quite a while. However, a credit card adjustment had been posted to the customer's account that was normally used to reverse a previous payment. This resulted in a "balance due" so the organization had sent a bill to the customer at the end of the month.

As the manager reviewed the supporting documentation, she realized the adjustment was probably incorrect because the documentation was referencing a transaction for a different customer.

That seemed like a silly, yet honest mistake, so she decided to review the actual credit card refund to see if any more information was available. She discovered that the refund was posted to a different credit card—not the one associated with the customer who received the bill.

But what puzzled her more was that her initials were used to approve the adjustment. However, she didn't remember making or approving the transaction. She thought to herself, *I've certainly messed up a customer account in the past, but how could we make two errors on one customer account?*

She kept looking at the credit card adjustment and realized other refunds had been posted to this particular credit card. She did a quick search for this credit card number and couldn't find that it had ever been used to purchase product from the bookstore.

Now she was intrigued. *Why are we making refunds to a credit card that we've never seen,* she wondered.

One by one, the manager started looking at the different refunds that had been posted to the anonymous credit card.

For every refund, she found a corresponding adjustment that was posted to a customer's account. The adjustments were made to look like the customer's previous credit card payment was being refunded. However, this also resulted in a balance due for the customer.

The manager grew suspicious. All the adjustments had her initials attached to the approval documents but she was positive she hadn't approved any of these adjustments.

Then the manager noticed something else tied to these refunds. A few days after the adjustments and credit card refunds were processed, another adjustment was posted to the customer's account that cleared the outstanding balance. This adjustment would "write-off" the remaining balance.

A bad-debt write-off was used when a customer with an outstanding balance could not be located, or refused to pay their bill. These were rarely used, and could only be authorized by the manager. Looking at these customer accounts, she knew that she didn't approve any of these write-off adjustments.

Now the manager was convinced something fraudulent was occurring; she also realized who the perpetrator was.

When the accounting clerk recovered from his illness and returned to work a few days later, the manager confronted him. With the mountain of evidence in front of him, he quickly admitted to the fraudulent scheme. He admitted that he would create fraudulent credit card adjustments and then post the refunds to his personal credit cards. Then, he would post a bad-debt write-off a few days later to clear the customer's outstanding balance and conceal his activity. He also admitted to forging the manager's initials approving the adjustments and write-offs.

In a four-month period, he initiated seven fraudulent transactions that resulted in almost five thousand dollars being posted to four personal credit cards.

The accounting clerk was terminated, and agreed to make restitution, in lieu of prosecution.

what went wrong

In this case study, several control weaknesses allowed the perpetrator to create fraudulent transactions and embezzle ministry funds, but the primary cause was poor segregation of duties. The accounting clerk had the ability to do several tasks that were incompatible when viewed through the lens of accountability.

The clerk was able to post adjustments to customer accounts, process refunds to credit cards and write-off bad debt. While some of the tasks were supposed to be reviewed and approved by the accounts receivable manager, the process was not controlled to make sure the manager saw every adjustment.

The manager would review printouts of the adjustments each day, but the clerk concealed his activity by destroying the printouts of his fake adjustments. The manager could have easily searched the electronic financial records for all adjustments to make sure she was reviewing and approving every adjustment, but she failed to do so.

She also failed to review and approve the credit card refunds. If she would have reviewed the credit card refunds, she would have noticed that the refunds were being posted to a different credit card than the one associated with the customer's account.

best practices

Billing schemes (which includes this type of refund fraud) are common schemes involving fraudulent disbursements of cash. A recent study found billing schemes make up 25 percent of all frauds, across all industries, involving asset misappropriation.[52] Billing schemes often last about twenty-four months before they are discovered, and result in a median loss of about one hundred thousand dollars.[53]

Unfortunately, religious and charitable organizations experience this type of fraud more often. This same study found billing schemes made up 52 percent of frauds at religious and charitable organizations.[54]

Thankfully for this ministry, this credit card refund scheme only lasted four months before it was discovered. Due to the accounting clerk's recent illness, he wasn't able to post the last write-off adjustment that would clear the customer's outstanding balance. As a result, when the monthly invoices were printed, this customer still had a balance, so an invoice was printed and included in the monthly mailing. The phone message from this customer was the only clue that something was amiss.

Poor segregation of duties is the breeding ground for fraudulent activity. Unfortunately, many churches and nonprofits do not separate financial responsibilities and have poor segregation of duties. As a result of incompatible duties, employees are more easily able to pull off embezzlement schemes like this credit card refund fraud.

However, the ministry in this case study did have multiple accounting staff and was able to separate financial responsibilities. Unfortunately, while the functions were split between the accounts receivable manager and the accounting clerk, a few more basic steps were needed to ensure all transactions were fully accountable and transparent.

If your church has a bookstore or coffee shop, or takes registrations for summer camps, retreats, or conferences, you have probably implemented some type of billing system for your church members and customers. And since credit cards are fast becoming the preferred choice for payment, this credit card refund scheme highlights the importance of having strong controls over the collection, billing, and adjustment of your customer accounts.

The most important control is separating the responsibilities for billing and collections. This will make it more difficult for one person to fraudulently process customer payments and conceal the activity by altering customer invoices or posting adjustments to customer accounts.

Consider implementing the following controls to reduce the risk of this fraud occurring at your ministry:

- Require at least two people to be involved in the billing and collections process.
- Require all adjustments and refunds to be supported with proper documentation.
- Require management approval for any adjustments to a customer's balance, including the write-off of bad debt.
- Require management approval before processing refunds.
- Make sure credit card refunds are posted to the original credit card used to make the purchase. If the card number is not available, send a check to the customer's address on file for the amount of the refund.

evaluate your organization

- ❏ Have you adequately separated the billing and collections process? Who performs these functions?
- ❏ Do you have separate individuals receiving payments, posting adjustments to customer accounts, and issuing credit card refunds? Who performs these functions?
- ❏ Do you require all adjustments and refunds to be supported with proper documentation? What constitutes proper documentation? What happens if documentation isn't available?

❑ Do you require management approval for any adjustments to a customer's balance? Who has authority to approve adjustments? How is approval documented?

❑ Do you require management approval when reducing a customer's accounts receivable balance? Who has authority to approve changes? How is approval documented?

❑ Do you require management approval before processing credit card refunds? Who has authority to approve refunds? How is approval documented?

❑ Do you post refunds to the same credit card used in the original transaction? If not, how do customers receive the refunds?

for further review

If you would like to assess the strength of your financial controls in this area, perform a mini-audit by following these steps:

1. Select ten customer accounts that have an accounts receivable balance.
2. Review the customers' account histories and look for any adjustments that were posted to their accounts.
3. Review the adjustments and evaluate whether the adjustments were properly supported, reviewed, and approved.

4. If any adjustments resulted in refunds, review the actual disbursement.

    a. Determine whether the refund was appropriately posted to the customer's credit card or mailed to the customer's address on file.

    b. If the check has already cleared the bank, review the canceled check to verify that it was written to the customer.

    c. Review the back of the check (if available) to see how the check was endorsed.

5. If your financial processes include the ability to post journal entries to the financial records, review any journal entries posted to the accounts receivable general ledger account in the past twelve months for proper support and approval. (An entry posted directly to this account may be an attempt to conceal improper activity.)

6. Research any unsupported adjustments, refunds or other questionable transactions.

Poor segregation of duties is the breeding ground for fraudulent activity.

UNPAID
PAYROLL
TAXES

The district officer looked at the twenty-three employees of the church and affiliated school gathered in the room and his heart sank. He wished there was another option for him, but he knew there was no other solution available. He opened the meeting with some pleasantries, and then proceeded to share the difficult news. "Due to mismanagement of church funds by the previous leadership," he began, "we have no other option but to close the church school and layoff all church and school employees immediately."

After the meeting, the district officer reflected that it was just a few months earlier when the phone on his desk rang. On the other end was the senior pastor of one of the churches in his district that he helped mentor. The pastor shared some discouraging news: The IRS had placed a lien on his church for unpaid payroll taxes. If the church didn't rectify the situation now, the IRS was threatening to close the church and the affiliated school for Kindergarten through grade 12. Unfortunately, the church didn't have the funds to pay the $400,000 tax bill and needed some help from the district office.

The pastor stated that he had no idea how this situation happened and explained that the church didn't have enough funds to pay their current bills, let alone the massive tax bill, and he didn't know where else to turn. To complicate matters, he stated that the bookkeeper had unexpectedly resigned.

The district officer agreed to visit the church to assess their situation. Knowing that the bookkeeper had just resigned, he brought an investigative team with him, including an accountant with experience in banking, auditing, and taxes. It didn't take long for the accountant to figure out the church had been properly withholding payroll taxes from their employees' wages, but failed to remit the taxes to the IRS. In fact, the church had been withholding taxes for the past six years without remitting them to the IRS. The church was submitting W-2 forms each year, but not a Form 941, so it didn't take the IRS very long to figure out the problem. The church soon began to receive notices of delinquency from the IRS that had continued for six years until the IRS finally took additional action and placed a lien on the church.

It was soon apparent to the district officer that the pastor was not only aware of the tax situation, but ordered it to happen. A review of the church financial records revealed that the pastor was spending more money than the church was receiving in contributions. He didn't allow the bookkeeper to remit the taxes to the IRS because he was spending the funds on other things. Further, the board was aware of the delinquent taxes because they often discussed it during board meetings.

Before the bookkeeper resigned, she tried to conceal her involvement in this scheme by destroying payroll documents and erasing a computer hard drive that contained the church's financial records. Fortunately, the investigative team was able to recover the financial records from the online backup provider and recreate the payroll documents.

The investigative team also discovered abuse in other financial areas. To hide the fact that he was hiring employees who were not eligible to work in the United States, the pastor had proxy or ghost employees on the payroll account. Each week, the church would pay these proxy employees, who would then cash the check and provide the funds to the person who actually worked at the church. The pastor also had a significant amount of expenses paid with a church credit card that were not supported with receipts or properly justified as a business expense. When the church's income could no longer cover his extravagant and excessive spending, he started transferring funds from the school to cover the church expenses. Unfortunately for him, the funds had run out, and the IRS got tired of waiting.

As a result of this abuse, the church had to close the school and send one hundred students to other schools. The church had to lay-off twenty-three employees of the church and school. The pastor and his wife lost their jobs and their home. It took another four months to pay off all the vendors.

Two years later, the church was still struggling to pay the tax bill, but had managed to move forward with a part-time secretary and a pro bono pastor. The former pastor and bookkeeper were still being investigated by the IRS for their involvement in this fraud.

what went wrong

In this case study, leaders entrusted to oversee the church finances failed to manage those finances responsibly and comply with applicable laws and regulations.

Several failures by leadership allowed this abuse to occur, which included:

- Failing to operate ethically in all aspects of church administration, including the hiring of employees.
- Failing to ensure applicable taxes were promptly remitted to the IRS.

- Failing to ensure required IRS Forms 941 were submitted to the IRS.
- Failing to create and execute a balanced budget for the church.
- Failing to hold the pastor and staff accountable for how funds were spent, including purchases made on church credit cards.

Most fraud cases are committed by sole perpetrators. One five-year study of fraud schemes found 86 percent were committed by one person.[55] Having several people involved, known as collusion, is rare. However, in this case, several people knew this deceit was occurring and colluded to keep it going, including the pastor, the bookkeeper, and the board members. Unfortunately, no one was willing to take their fiduciary responsibilities seriously and put a stop to this scheme. In the end, many innocent people suffered the consequences of their leaders' misconduct.

best practices

Payroll tax reporting can be confusing. Regardless of whether an organization is for-profit or not-for-profit, the IRS has several reporting requirements for organizations with employees. For example, employers must withhold federal income taxes and Social Security taxes from their employee's wages and deposit those taxes with the IRS. For smaller organizations, taxes are submitted monthly, but for larger organizations, the payroll taxes must be remitted to the IRS on a weekly basis. Additionally, employers must file quarterly tax returns (Form 941) and issue annual Wage and Tax Statements (Form W-2) to employees.

Employees must complete the Employee's Withholding Allowance Certificate (Form W-4) to claim withholding allowances, which determines the amount of income tax that should be withheld from their wages.

Further, when hiring employees, the government requires employers to verify that the employee is eligible to work in the United States. For any employee hired after November 6, 1986, an Employment Eligibility Verification (Form I-9) should be completed.

Most churches are subject to the withholding requirements, but some exceptions exist for ministerial staff, which only contributes to the confusion. For example, ministers are treated as employees for federal tax reporting, but are exempt from federal tax withholding. However, if they would like to have federal taxes voluntarily withheld by the church, they should fill out a W-4 form.

Because payroll can be so confusing, some churches outsource their payroll process to a local accounting firm or third-party payroll provider. However, the church is still responsible to make sure payroll taxes are properly remitted to the IRS. One fraudulent payroll service in New York collected over $3 million in payroll taxes from 1,100 small businesses and non-profits but failed to remit the taxes to the IRS. Instead, the president used the funds for operating expenses and personal expenditures.[56,57] While he was sentenced to eight years in prison and ordered to make restitution, his clients are still liable for the unpaid taxes.[58]

To make sure your payroll taxes are properly deposited with the IRS, employers can sign up for the Treasury Department's

Electronic Federal Tax Payment Service at https://www.eftps.gov/ eftps/. This free service allows users to go online to pay taxes or see what tax deposits have been made. Whether you handle your own payroll, or outsource it, visiting this website should be a part of your monthly internal control process.

While it may seem the IRS has too many regulations, they do offer a wealth of information to help nonprofits navigate the vast sea of requirements. They have a website dedicated to churches and other religious organizations, covering a wide range of topics that includes a quick reference tax guide, details about annual filing requirements, and a discussion on prohibited activities and unrelated business income tax. If you want to know more about these topics, visit their website at http://www.irs.gov/Charities-&-Non-Profits/Churches-&-Religious-Organizations.

evaluate your organization

❑ Do you have a properly completed and signed Forms I-9 and W-4 for each employee?

❑ Do you remit payroll taxes promptly? Who performs this function?

❑ Do you submit IRS Form 941 quarterly? Who performs this function?

❑ Do you operate within a balanced budget? How often is financial activity reviewed? Who is responsible to manage and oversee financial activity?

❑ Does someone not involved in the payroll process ensure payroll taxes are deposited and required forms are submitted? Who performs this review? How often?

for further review

If you would like to assess the strength of your financial controls in this area, perform a mini-audit by following these steps:

1. Review each employee's personnel file. Determine whether a properly completed Form W-4 and I-9 is on file for each employee. Ensure each form is properly dated and signed.
2. Review the Form 941 submissions for the last two years. Evaluate the completeness of each submission by tracing the figures on the report to applicable payroll reports for the same period.
3. Sign up with the Treasury Department's Electronic Federal Tax Payment System. Assign someone not involved in the payroll process to visit the system on a regular basis to make sure tax deposits are being made.

Unfortunately, no one was

willing to take their fiduciary

responsibilities seriously and

put a stop to this scheme.

endnotes

[1]Associated Press, "Father and Son Pastors Plead Guilty to Stealing $3.1 M From Church," FoxNews.com, June 15, 2009, accessed September 26, 2013, http://www.foxnews.com/story/2009/06/15/father-and-son-pastors-plead-guilty-to-stealing-31-m-from-church/.

[2]"Former Central Texas Minister Sentenced In $700,000 Theft," KWTX.com, October 1, 2008, accessed September 26, 2013, http://www.kwtx.com/news/headlines/30183349.html.

[3]Samuel Smith, "BGCT reports $1.3M fraud, mismanagement in church funds," BPNews.net, November 1, 2006, accessed September 26, 2013, http://www.bpnews.net/bpnews.asp?ID=24299.

[4]Association of Certified Fraud Examiners, *Report to the Nations on Occupational Fraud and Abuse: 2012 Global Fraud Study*, 2, 25, accessed May 23, 2013, http://www.acfe.com/uploadedFiles/ACFE_Website/Content/rttn/2012-report-to-nations.pdf.

[5]Association of Certified Fraud Examiners, *Report to the Nations*, 4.

[6]Ibid., 25.

[7]Internal Revenue Service, *Internal Revenue Service Fiscal Year 2012 Enforcement and Service Results*, 7, accessed July 26, 2013, http://www.irs.gov/uac/Newsroom/FY-2012-Enforcement-and-Service-Results.

[8]The United States Senate Committee on Finance, "Grassley Releases Review of Tax Issues Raised by Media-based Ministries," January 6, 2011, accessed April 14, 2011, http://www.finance.senate.gov/newsroom/ranking/release/?id=5fa343ed-87eb-49b0-82b9-28a9502910f7.

[9]Warren Bird, *The Economic Outlook of Very Large Churches* (Leadership Network, 2013), 3, accessed February 20, 2013, http://www.leadnet.org/resources/download/the_economic_outlook_of_very_large_churches_pdf.

[10]Christopher T. Marquet, *The 2012 Marquet Report on Embezzlement* (Marquet International, 2013), 18, accessed June 3, 2013, http://www.marquetinternational.com/pdf/the_2012_marquet_report_on_embezzlement.pdf.

[11]Association of Certified Fraud Examiners, *Report to the Nations*, 57.

[12]Assemblies of God USA, "Our Mission & Core Values," last modified February 26, 2010, accessed July 29, 2013, http://www.ag.org/top/About/mission.cfm.

[13]KPMG LLP, *Who is the Typical Fraudster?*, 10, accessed February 20, 2013, http://www.kpmg.com/US/en/IssuesAndInsights/ArticlesPublications/Documents/who-is-the-typical-fraudster.PDF.

[14]Ibid., 15–16.

[15]Ibid., 10, 13.

[16]Association of Certified Fraud Examiners, *Report to the Nations*, 4-5.

[17]Ibid., 25.

[18]Ibid., 25, 29.

[19]Ibid., 4.

[20]Ibid.

[21]Ibid., 14.

[22]Ibid.

[23]Ibid., 5.

[24]National Center For Charitable Statistics, "Quick Facts About Nonprofits," accessed July 29, 2013, http://www.nccs.urban.org/statistics/quickfacts.cfm.

[25]David K. Shipler, "Reagan and Gorbachev Sign Missile Treaty and Vow to Work for Greater Reductions," NYTimes.com, December 9, 1987, accessed August 24, 2013, http://www.nytimes.com/1987/12/09/politics/09REAG.html?pagewanted=2&pagewanted=all&smid=pl-share.

[26]COSO is an acronym for the Committee of Sponsoring Organizations for the Commission on Fraudulent Financial Reporting (Treadway Commission).

[27]Kurt F. Reding et al., *Internal Auditing: Assurance & Consulting Services* (Altamonte Springs, FL: The Institute of Internal Auditors Research Foundation, 2007), 5–8.

[28]Paul Payne, "Guerneville Woman Takes Plea Bargain in Church Embezzlement Case," PressDemocrat.com, March 12, 2012, accessed July 29, 2013, http://www.pressdemocrat.com/article/20120312/articles/120319932?tc=ar.

[29]Sharon Otterman and Russ Buettner, "In Million-Dollar Theft Case, Church Worker With a Secret Past," NYTimes.com, January 30, 2012, accessed July 29, 2013, http://www.nytimes.com/2012/01/31/nyregion/new-york-archdiocese-bookkeeper-charged-with-stealing-1-million.html?_r=4&pagewanted=all&.

[30]Federal Bureau of Investigation, "Former American Diabetes Financial Analyst Pleads Guilty to Embezzling Nearly $570,000," FBI Washington Field Office, September 23, 2011, accessed July 29, 2013, http://www.fbi. gov/washingtondc/press-releases/2011/former-american-diabetes-financial-analyst-pleads-guilty-to-embezzling-nearly-570-000.

[31]Jeff German, "Former Las Vegas Church Treasurer Faces Fraud Charges," ReviewJournal.com, September 6, 2012, accessed June 10, 2013, http://www. reviewjournal.com/news/crime-courts/former-las-vegas-church-treasurer-faces-fraud-charges.

[32]Richard R. Hammar, "If an Embezzler Confesses," *Managing Your Church Blog*, August 11, 2011, accessed August 26, 2011, http://www.blog. managingyourchurch.com/2011/08/if_an_embezzler_confesses.html.

[33]Richard R. Hammar, "How Do We Confront Suspected Embezzlement?" ChurchLawandTax.com, accessed December 21, 2011, http://www. churchlawandtax.com/private/library/viewarticle.php?aid=118.

[34]Ibid.

[35]Association of Certified Fraud Examiners, *Report to the Nations*, 4.

[36]Ibid., 61, 63.

[37]Ibid., 62.

[38]Ibid., 63.

[39]Ibid., 61.

[40]Ibid., 62.

[41]Evangelical Council for Financial Accountability, "ECFA Mission Statement," accessed August 28, 2013, http://www.ecfa.org/Content/MissionStatement.

[42]Association of Certified Fraud Examiners, *Report to the Nations*, 12-13.

[43]KPMG, *Who is the Typical Fraudster?*, 10.

[44]Ibid.

[45]Federal Bureau of Investigation, "Head of Charter School Pleads Guilty to Fraud Charges," FBI Philadelphia Division, August 13, 2013, accessed August 13, 2013, http://www.fbi.gov/philadelphia/press-releases/2013/head-of-charter-school-pleads-guilty-to-fraud-charges.

[46]The names of the organization and individuals involved have been changed to protect their identities.

[47]Federal Bureau of Investigation, "Bookkeeper Sentenced to Prison for Fraud and Aggravated Identity Theft," FBI Birmingham Division, April 3, 2013, accessed April 3, 2013, http://www.fbi.gov/birmingham/press-releases/2013/bookkeeper-sentenced-to-prison-for-fraud-and-aggravated-identity-theft.

[48]Marquet, *2012 Marquet Report*, 5.

[49]Association of Certified Fraud Examiners, *Report to the Nations*, 31.

[50]Federal Bureau of Investigation, "Former American Diabetes Financial Analyst Pleads Guilty."

[51]Federal Bureau of Investigation, "Landover Woman Indicted for Allegedly Embezzling More Than $453,000 from Her Employer," FBI Baltimore Division, April 29, 2013, accessed July 29, 2013, http://www.fbi.gov/baltimore/press-releases/2013/landover-woman-indicted-for-allegedly-embezzling-more-than-453-000-from-her-employer.

[52]Association of Certified Fraud Examiners, *Report to the Nations*, 12.

[53]Ibid., 12–13.

[54]Ibid., 31.

[55]Marquet, *2012 Marquet Report*, 13.

[56]Will Astor, "Plea sets payback by Sykes," RBJ.net, November 4, 2011, accessed September 26, 2013, http://www.rbj.net/print_article.asp?aID=189432.

[57]"Federal money laundering, tax fraud charges," SteubenCourier.com, October 11, 2011, accessed September 26, 2013, http://www.steubencourier.com/x1138515272/Federal-money-laundering-tax-fraud-charges.

[58]Internal Revenue Service, "Examples of Employment Tax Fraud Investigations—Fiscal Year 2012," updated September 17, 2013, accessed September 26, 2013, http://www.irs.gov/uac/Examples-of-Employment-Tax-Fraud-Investigations-Fiscal-Year-2012.